Healing with Qualities

ALSO BY MANUEL SCHOCH

Journal of Active Meditations
Journal of Interviews with Manuel Schoch
The Little Book of Time Therapy
The Wisdom of Time Therapy

With Love

Healing with Qualities

The Essence of Time Therapy

Manuel Schoch

SENTIENT PUBLICATIONS, LLC

First Sentient Publications edition 2005
Copyright © 2005 by Manuel Schoch

A paperback original

Printed in the United States of America

Cover design by Kim Johansen, Black Dog Design
Book design by Edition Spuren

Library of Congress Cataloging-in-Publication Data

Schoch, Manuel, 1946-
Healing with qualities : the essence of time therapy / Manuel Schoch.—
1st ed.
p. cm.
ISBN 1-59181-031-0
1. Healing. 2. Time—Psychological aspects. 3. Ego (Psychology)
I. Title.
RZ999.S367 2004
615.8'51—dc22   2004014111

SENTIENT PUBLICATIONS
A Limited Liability Company
1113 Spruce Street
Boulder, CO 80302
www.sentientpublications.com

Contents

Introduction

If you have picked up this book the chances are that you have sought help from a psychotherapist, counsellor or healer of some kind at some time in your life. You may have tried some of the many "self-help" treatments and therapies now available on the market in an effort to improve the quality of your life or deal with a particular problem. There are many reasons for this, and for those of us who seek psychological help there are three main methods used by professional helpers to help us feel better about our everyday lives, reduce our stress levels and have happier relationships.

One method is to delve into the past to try and unearth the origins of our neuroses, complexes or traumas that lie hidden in the happenings of childhood or infancy, or even further back in past lives. The second is to fill our lives with constructive, creative activities and develop a "positive mental attitude" to help drive out the undesirable elements in our behavior, such as addiction or depression. The third, which is part of the evolution of human consciousness toward seeing "the whole person" as a spiritual as well as a physical, emotional and mental being, is to consciously bring in the power of the soul. The power of the soul influences the brain via the mind, and consequently all aspects of a person's nature. We are at last discovering how to integrate Eastern and Western understandings of the psyche, and there are now various psychotherapeutic approaches that use the wisdom and teachings of

Buddhism and the Tao, for example, to develop new ways to help us make peace with our past and free up our potential in the future.

The two main forms I now work with are Time Therapy and Out-of-Body Healing. Out-of-Body Healing involves projecting energy outward away from the body. Time Therapy helps us deal with psychological problems and fears not by analyzing them or by looking to the past for explanations, or by resisting or being against our weaknesses and deep feelings of sadness. Instead, we try to stay with these feelings and learn to observe them without reaction, description or interpretation. When we can do this, we create a relationship to our qualities and the possibility then of real transformation.

Sadness is the key to love and to health. It offers an effective way of helping us deal differently with a range of common problems that affect many of us today including addictions, aggression, depression, mental stress and tension, feelings of frustration, isolation, hurt, rejection and the whole area of relationships. You have to change nothing.

In the older forms of therapy the focus is on what is not good in yourself, while in Time Therapy we focus on our potential. Jealousy, fear or anger are yours only if you give them a history. Feelings like these are natural, but if we understand the process of each one it is possible to deal with it instead of just living with it. In order to do this we have to let go of what we call the ego, the sense of self that we call "I". There is more to us than the mind, as the mystics believed. Time Therapy is based not only on the observation of the mind-body level but also of the aura structure, the energy system, the energy body and soul qualities. The quality aura is consciousness, potential and the future. When this is contacted through simple awareness it permeates the entire aura structure and we become fully human, an expression of the sacred in the ordinary world. We are able to live in a state of happiness, when consciousness – the qualities – are manifested through body, mind and aura.

In this book we will begin with an exploration of whether we can really solve our problems through understanding our past and whether it is even true that the past plays the dominant role we give to it. It is difficult for the mind to deal with these questions as the mind is structured in time, so it cannot really understand, for example, that the future is more important than the past. Intellectually, it is impossible for the mind to grasp this, although in terms of energy it is obvious and understandable. The intellect, which is something that is born then moves from one point in time to the other and finally dies, lacks this understanding.

The first thing a child of two or three years old understands in connection to *time* is the so-called *now*. The next step in understanding time for a little child of this age is the future. Any understanding of the past occurs at the very end of childhood. This is highly significant. Why do all little children first grasp the so-called now? Having an understanding of only the now means that they cannot abstract toward a future or past.

If we observe ourselves carefully we can see how the movement of energy is always a movement toward something new. In scientific terms, we would call this process *evolution*. For thousands of years, mystics such as Socrates have said that you have to know yourself. What exactly did they mean by *know yourself*? If knowing yourself means only to know your history, you are limiting yourself tremendously. If knowing yourself means to only understand your past actions, then you are once again limiting yourself. These options leave no possibility for the movement of growth and flexibility that is necessary for healthy living. It does not take into account your aura or your qualities, which we will explore in more detail later.

To begin with, knowing yourself may involve the process of seeing where you came from just so that you can let go of this and move forward. There is a beautiful paradox here: while fear is always directed toward the future, that which haunts us and which creates a fear

of being haunted is derived from the past. Religions (not religious people) and the church establishment have used this to create and maintain their power base by saying that if you are sinful, you will be haunted
by your sins. They define what is good or bad and insist that you go to
church and obey certain rules so that you may then go to heaven. Traditional psychology, on the other hand, insists that you need to change
and understand what went wrong with your past in order to reach self-
fulfillment.

Socrates simply encouraged you to know yourself. Knowing yourself
in this sense includes the past and all of your potential, which represents the future. In this movement of knowing yourself you are released from being haunted by the past. Analyzing the past and thinking that you are the way you are because of specific incidents in your
past merely creates a movement of blaming or of giving away the responsibility for why you are the way you are, which limits your freedom to be. In going down this route you will never know yourself, and
you will always be concerned with that which haunts you. It becomes
an invented ghost that will be with you for the rest of your life, and if
anyone wanted to have power and control over you they could use this
aspect of your past as leverage.

Each one of us, even the most enlightened, can always fail. This is
beautifully described in the Bible in the description of how Jesus is
tempted in the desert. In order for you to change you have to aspire to
be different from how you are now. As perfection is an impossible goal
to attain, you will therefore always be dogged by what is not right in
you. What Socrates meant is that if you see yourself, which really means
to have a relationship to yourself, then no one can haunt you or claim
responsibility for who you are. For as long as you hold someone else
responsible for who you are, whether it is your mother or your father,
you have nowhere to go from there; you are simply not in freedom.

Freedom does not come through escaping – thinking that it does is a
spiritual fantasy, and much of the current new age movement is simply a

modern form of escapism. In encouraging indulgence in ideas about past lives, for example, it fulfills a similar role to the Christian church, which encouraged us to escape into beliefs about heaven and hell.

True freedom comes through knowing yourself, and this does not involve having to change anything. All that is needed is to see what has been, without reacting to it in any way and in so doing, putting an end to the story there. As you begin to read and use this book, try to see it not as an intellectual exercise but as an opportunity to learn a new way of thinking, change your perspective, begin to realize your potential and connect with the qualities which are the real essence of your being.

CHAPTER 1

The Body Is Form, the Ego Is Time

The body as form

When a child is born the first thing it becomes aware of is the body. The first thing you are in touch with and can identify with is your body and how it is: whether it is hot or cold, comfortable or uncomfortable, hungry or full, tired or awake. This is a very simple, natural movement, and you quickly learn that your body plays an important role in your sense of well-being. You discover fairly early on that your body is form and that it has boundaries.

In research involving babies and young children between the ages of 18 months to two years of age, it has been observed how they come to realize that the boundary formed by the body is separate from the rest of the world and that there is a distinction between your body and mine. At this point we have our first glimpse of consciousness.

As a direct consequence of this realization, the child sees that the body, which is form, can be carried around by itself and at one moment can be in connection with its mother and in the next on its own again. As all parents will know, by three years old the child becomes stubborn. At this stage in its growth the child experiences how its body can be independent of its mother, and this is simply a natural progression in developing freedom of will. It is a beautiful manifestation of consciousness starting to flower. Parents usually react to this stubbornness based on a fear of having their authority undermined and a desire to discourage such behavior, but in fact this phase is essential if a child is going to develop a sense of freedom.

Between the ages of two and three, the child realizes that not only does it have a physical body that can move independently, that has boundaries, an inside and an outside, but there is also the capacity to reflect, to start to feel. In this way the *I* or *ego* is born.

The ego as time

Without the ego we could not operate in the world, and from this point on we begin to construct our ego or sense of self based on our experiences and responses in different situations. The child has learned that the body has boundaries that need to be maintained and defended. When we begin to think and feel and to want to have this or that, we try to defend the boundaries of the ego or the I in the same way. This is done through the associative thought processes, which we will come to later, but at this level of existence if the body is form, then the next level, the I or ego, must also be form. It seems obvious. However, the ego has to do with time and not form. The child, however cannot see this; it does not experience the ego as time but as form instead.

As we continue to build up our ego as something that is solid or in form, our behavior becomes conditioned by our sense of who we think we are, our self-perception, our likes and dislikes, our fears and beliefs, our experiences in relationship with others and in the world. In the first type of conditioned behavior there is the familiar *fight or flight* response. Whenever confronted by danger, or what we perceive as danger, we either fight or escape, or if neither of these is possible, we freeze and become immobile, like a mouse might behave when there is no escape from the jaws of a cat. The brain functions in this way whenever there is even a minor threat; it immediately tries to access one of these responses and it has a tendency to react in this way even with psychological problems, which do not pose any real threat to our safety.

The next type of behavior has to do with learning. Like the human brain, the brain of animals is designed to learn not only according to the Darwinian evolutionary model but also through the out-of-body conscious learning. The *hundred monkeys* experiment showed that if a group of monkeys was shown how to pick potatoes in a certain way, a few months later the same type of monkey somewhere else in the world would be able to do the same. Learning is often seen as a process of analyzing your mistakes and then doing things differently using these experiences. Real learning, however, involves a movement of being ready to see a mistake and leave it at that or to forget it. Learning has to do with not judging yourself. When a baby tries to stand but keeps falling over, it does not then sit down to analyze what went wrong or whether it tried hard enough; it just keeps trying over and over again.

The moment we start judging our learning, our energy gets diverted into questioning or worrying about our progress. Because the brain cannot make the distinction between reality and a thought, it will then sense that there is a problem and immediately begin to try to solve it, so more energy is absorbed and the brain becomes less vital. At birth, unless the brain is damaged it is totally awake and brilliant, but so much fear is created around how one should learn that children are put under great pressure to learn in what is seen as the right way. So to forget means to learn without judging or focusing on one's weaknesses. In paying too much attention and trying to understand our weak points, we simply give them more energy because the brain will become mobilized into thinking that something has to be done and will lose its intelligence. Fixating on our weaknesses causes unnecessary problems and lack of freedom.

Freedom and insecurity

Where there is no freedom there is insecurity in the negative sense of the word. The opposite of security is not insecurity but freedom. A mind that wants security creates limitation, and the brain is then constantly fighting the limitation. Learning is the movement of always being totally insecure about what will happen next.

The third type of behavior has nothing to do with childhood or culture and is present in the brain from the moment we are born. In religious contexts it is referred to as longing but more usually as simple curiosity. It can best be seen in children. For example, a two-year-old wants to find out more about something by the fireplace. As you know the fireplace can be dangerous you tell the child not to go near it. The child gives you a strange look but continues to move toward it. You mistakenly think that the child is deliberately disobeying you instead of realizing that it is simply curious. On the level of biological consciousness, curiosity is stronger than love.

And the will may be important, but fantasy or curiosity is always the stronger urge. It involves being totally ready to move outward, away from safety, even if it jeopardizes one's own life. Such is the intelligence of evolution; consciousness is not possible without curiosity and learning.

Creativity is a symptom or flowering of curiosity, yet the mind prefers to cling to the past or to focus on one's weaknesses in an attempt to find security or stability in the idea of being someone, to have an identity, to be secure in knowing who you are.

Form and time

If parents then deal with this situation in the same manner as the child is dealing with it, i.e. if you fight the stubbornness, which means fighting the will of the child, inevitably you end up fighting against their sense of freedom and battling with the child's development in terms of its body consciousness and ego consciousness. It will be difficult then for the child to learn that the I is of time. It will instead structure it more and more as form. If we look at the significance of our past experience in shaping who we are now, what happens to you between twelve to seventeen years of age often has more of an impact than the first few years of life. During this stage of puberty there is a possibility for a whole new shift in perspective to begin. If the I at this point cannot shift to a time-based perspective, then the energy of a person will be progressively shunted away in all sorts of other directions. The I will not be able to realize that it is more than form. It may only have momentary glimpses of timelessness.

For example, as children, we all had moments when we were totally absorbed in our actions. This movement of being totally absorbed in action with total awareness means losing that sense of time – when your body and ego are melting into something beyond duality.

It is easy to know when you are immersed in awareness, as the less awareness one has, then the more time (that is, the subjective feeling of time) one experiences. By this I mean *living* time as opposed to *cycle* or *phase* time. Cycle time relates to the twenty-four hours on a clock, whereas living time is what you experience; it is relative time.

We cannot discern our potential if we are constantly concerned with the body/form or absorbing energy in fighting it in some way with the ego/ I. When we do this, energy gets absorbed not only in the body but also in the illusion that the I is also form when in fact the I is time. If at the age of seventeen we could see that the I is much more than form, we would then become spiritual. However, if this does not happen at seventeen, then usually we have to wait until the age of fifty. As Jung observed, fifty years of age is when the spiritual or religious impulse returns in all of us. If there is much more to the I than we think, what can we find out by seeing or being aware that it is time and not form?

The future becomes the past

The Buddha taught that if you focus on that which will not survive, on that which will pass away, you are focusing on the wrong thing. Time is the movement of something passing away. The moment you reach the future it becomes the past. The future is the unknown and involves fear, and the moment you are faced with fear you are in the past. So in terms of cause and effect, the future is really the cause. This may be difficult to understand because we have been conditioned to believe in "cause and effect," but it is worth trying to understand it in this way.

The Buddha advised us not to cling to the known or to that which dies because the known is always going to die. Modern psychologists encourage us not to cling to the ego and not to try to understand that which is at any rate always changing. How can you understand something that is constantly changing? How can you hope to solve your problems by looking at that which has created the problem and is the problem? The mind strongly believes that it can change itself through understanding itself. But if the "I" is an illusion based on time, it cannot do this.

Coming back to the question of why it is so difficult to see with the mind that the future is the cause, that the future creates the past, this is because the mind can never be in the future; it is always in the past. It is always with that which has in fact already happened, and therefore it is always the cause of blockage of energy. If you then insist with your will (which is still of the mind) to move into the future, you are effectively instructing the mind to commit suicide.

This is supported by the Eastern religious concepts that claim that you can only become enlightened when you are no longer preoccupied with your past and also by the most important principle in Christianity – the act of forgiveness. What is the movement of *forgiveness*? It is the movement of absolutely and totally cutting yourself off from the past and leaving it behind you. We do not seem to live like this at all, and Christianity as a religion certainly does not encourage us to do so. We live within the *shoulds* of Christianity, which again simply absorbs energy.

By now you may be saying fine, I can understand this, but how do I actually deal with this because at the biological level I need the ego. Indeed on the level of biological consciousness that includes the body and part of the thinking apparatus provided by the brain, you do need it.

There is also a biopsychological level of consciousness where you also need the I, because it is on this level that your memory functions, and you do need memory; for example, after having learned how to drive a car you need to remember how to do it again the following day. But there is also the level of psychospiritual consciousness, and all the laws are different here. Newton's laws are not wrong just because they were followed by Einstein's theories; for example, they are each valid at different levels of analysis.

So the mind struggles with how to approach this. It can see that to work with the I is useless, and it can also see that the I is the problem, but it cannot find a way out of the puzzle. For as long as you are connected with the I, and as the I is time, you will not understand what time means. This is because the I cannot examine itself. The same process occurs when you really change, that is, when true transformation takes place. You will not be aware of it until after the event, and even then only upon reflection. If you were to be aware of transforming during the process itself, then half of your available energy would be absorbed in that awareness, limiting the process. So do not expect to be aware of change as it is occurring, as no change is possible if you are constantly observing and watching for it. The I cannot see what time is for as long as it is dominating consciousness; however, it persists in wanting to know how it can facilitate change.

If only there were a simple answer to this, the world would already be a paradise. There are, however, some hints and suggestions to guide you through this process.

CHAPTER 2

The Future Creates the Past

Analyzing the past

The art of reaching true freedom can only be practiced effectively if we understand the structure of what we call the future. As long as we define reality as being dependent on the past we can never be free. By analyzing the past we may succeed in altering our behavior slightly, but not much more than that. For example, if you feel jealous and want to put an end to your feelings of jealousy, you ask why you are jealous. The feeling of jealousy arises out of the belief that you are not loved as much as someone else. You may then come to the conclusion, rightly or wrongly, that your mother did not love you enough as a child, and now you are possessed by the fear of not being loved enough.

Once you know this intellectually it may ease your jealousy, and you may even find that you seem a little less jealous, but does this really give you freedom? You are still dependent on understanding your problem based on your relationship with your mother. Your life may change a little as a result of understanding your tendency toward jealousy; you might be able to control your jealous feelings in the future, but is this enough? How can you have quality of life, how can you use your potential if you are not free? First of all, we need to look at the word *future*. Every word is a description, and every word is also a process.

The word *future* as a process is the movement of hope and fear. This is not about biological fears that result from not having enough food and shelter, or being fearful when someone is about to attack you physically; it is about psychospiritual fears, for example, the fear that somewhere out there, something is against you; or the fear of not being sure whether you can deal with what is new – fear of the unknown.

Fear, hope and desire

When this kind of psychological fear becomes dominant in our lives, one of the ways we try to deal with it is by nurturing the notion of hope. Hoping that you will manage in the future is a typical psychological structure around which we make statements like "once I have understood myself better, once I have worked though all my problems, then I will be able to have a good relationship," for example.

But as Jesus said, if you search for heaven up there, you will never find it as the birds will be there before you, and if you search for heaven in the ocean, you will never find it there either because the fish will be there before you. Hope is not the same as confidence and trust because it embodies the future, and this tends to create a vicious circle. Accompanying hope usually is the fear of not getting what you want, and so you are then brought back again to fear.

Fear together with hope creates desire. The Buddha said, "Be without desire and you immediately become enlightened." Desire or wanting is the movement of hope or of wishing for something, coupled with the fear that it may never be realized. The Buddha also said that whenever you have a goal you wish to attain, once again you create a problem for yourself. In trying to achieve that goal you have to split your energy into two: one part will be attempting to move toward the goal or to fulfill the desire, while the other part of your energy is used up in constantly watching and asking from the position of fear whether or not you are going to succeed; the result is duality, misery and conflict.

As we can see, this preoccupation with the future is the cause of much misery. In response to this statement the mind says this is impossible because logically and intellectually it can only see any cause as arising from the past. Intellectually, this may seem to be the case. If you were to say to someone working in quantum physics that light is not the fastest form of information and that there is something that is even faster than light, they would reply from an intellectual standpoint that this is impossible.

Energy and the future

Fear of the future, together with hope and desire – which are all the same – block energy regardless of how the fear may have arisen. As soon as consciousness arises (and this is a natural part of evolution), a sense of the future is created automatically. A movement toward something unknown naturally creates fear, hope, wishes and desires. There is nothing wrong with all of this; however, it does result in diversions to the overall flow of energy.

Imagine a little girl whose mother and father have an easy life with no struggle for survival or existence. They have their own little quarrels or insecurities, but they love their child. Like all of us they make mistakes, but there can be no education or learning without making some mistakes. Mistakes are created when feelings are expressed – whenever someone says or does something to you, it creates a feeling within you to which you react. Even if you are the most loving person, sometimes you may react in inappropriate ways toward your child. For example, when our son Fabbi, who is a very sensitive boy, was six months old, he was playing in bed between my wife and myself. A picture suddenly fell down from the wall behind him and I shrieked. My son thought I was screaming at him, and he immediately reacted with shock. He was terribly upset. So you see, even if you love your child, it is possible that your child may misunderstand something you do or say. For a moment, their aura system or energy field will be shattered and shaken. Going back to our story of the girl, her temperament or character is very quiet. By the time she is twelve months old, one could even say that she is quite shy. The quality associated with shyness is of not always assuming that one knows everything there is to know. It is a beautiful quality, but of course it can also be a hindrance if it is overly manifest. By the time this girl is two years old, her parents, who naturally want the best for their child, begin to wonder what they can do to help her overcome her shyness so that she might have more contact with people. They tell her to go and play a little more, or to do a little more of this or a little more of that. Even worse, they may even consider sending the poor girl to therapy at five years old.

This child soon starts to think that maybe there is something wrong with her feelings of shyness, and she begins to think about being more outgoing and about being more in touch with people. Soon she begins to believe that there is something wrong in being shy. In time, even if the parents disguise their feelings about her shyness, the girl will say to herself that the shyness is somehow a hindrance to being in contact with others in a social context. Shyness does have its drawbacks; for instance, when invited to parties you feel uneasy when you first arrive, and you lack confidence in knowing how to move or behave toward people.

To some extent this girl's shyness was created by her parents because they too are shy, but regardless of what created the problem, between fourteen and seventeen years of age the girl will develop a problem with this quality, and she will begin to fight it. How does one usually deal with this or any other problem?

The limits of understanding
A problem is always nothing other than the movement of being hurt. What makes us then start to fight our problem, in the case of this example, of shyness? As with every other psychological problem, seeing it as a barrier to future happiness and well-being necessitates finding a way of getting rid of it. This is the usual way of dealing with our problems.

So the girl begins to try to understand her shyness, and this means that her energy becomes focused on the problem. By focusing her energy on the problem there is automatically less energy available to do anything else; a blockage or slowing down of energy is created, part of the energy system becomes deficient in its flow of energy and therefore cannot function normally. At the same time another part of the energy system, on the level of consciousness, is always focused and directed toward the future and is locked in the remembrance of how the shyness hinders her from having a relationship. The third part is locked in continually observing whether or not there has been any significant change.

What is actually taking place here? Part of her whole energy system will be blocked on the level of the body, which is something like having a car parked in the garage unused. It will be blocked on the level of consciousness, and therefore consciousness becomes limited. It will also be blocked on the level of action, so there is no longer any real action. When this happens, in the worst possible case a person might become completely paralyzed, as they are left with no perspective whatsoever.

Energy and transformation
Every problem that you try to solve by understanding and analyszing creates a blockage or diversion of your energies and therefore limits your perspective even more. It does not matter where the problem originated from or when it started. The act of trying to solve it immediately limits your possibilities or your potential for change. It creates a breakup in the otherwise unified flow of energy.

When you admit to having a problem, you are automatically describing the process of feeling hurt. What then happens in terms of energy when you decide to seek therapy because of a desire to get rid of this problem? The therapist may tell you the only way you can get rid of your problem is by "loving yourself." How can you realistically love yourself if you are busy wanting to get rid of a part of you?

This need to improve yourself then absorbs part of your energy. If you start off with 100 percent energy, 50 percent is used up in being self-critical and preoccupied with that which you want to get rid of. Of the remaining 50 percent, there will be a part that is involved in making an effort to understand how you may effect this change and another part that is constantly observing whether or not any change has happened. There is yet another part that is involved in self-justification over why you may not have changed as yet. How much energy can there be left for real transformation? It is exactly because of these blockages and creating conflict that the girl we described earlier may not be able to enter into a meaningful relationship.

The future creates the past

In this way the preoccupation with the future is the cause of a lot of our problems. By seeing things a little differently, we can begin to realize how it is the future that creates the past. The girl has diverted her energy into many different routes. It does not matter how or why the shyness was created. Labelling her mother as the cause is not helpful in assisting her in overcoming her shyness.

It is helpful to know that the shyness is simply temperament and that it exists not because there is anything intrinsically wrong. Looking into the past will show how shyness as a process develops, not in order to find someone to blame or take responsibility for it but simply as an unfolding of a process of realization. The attribute of shyness is shared by millions of people independent of their education or upbringing, and this is because shyness is part of an impersonal structure.

In our example, the girl fights her shyness as a result of focusing on the future, which in turn blocks the flow of her energy. The girl can therefore never develop a relationship to this shyness, and it is exactly this movement toward the future full of all its fear that creates the situation of never having a meaningful emotional relationship. When she looks back on her life, she will comment on how she never had a relationship because of her shyness. The future has therefore created her history or, in other words, her past. It is how she has dealt with the future, with her desires, hopes and fears, which has unwittingly created her past.

Does the present exist?

So far, it is possible to see that the future always contains the past, but the past never contains the future. What then is the concept of the *now*, the so-called *present*? You have probably heard the saying that you should not live in the past nor in the future but always in the present. This sound logical, but does the now really exist? Take breathing as an example. Let's say that breathing in represents the future while breathing out is the past, and the pauses in between represent the present. How long can you breathe in for, how long can you breathe out for and for how long can you stop breathing? It is actually impossible to keep breathing in without breathing out. The now is really when awareness becomes narrowed to that tiny movement between the past and the future.

We have three kinds of memory in the brain. One is the ultra short-term memory, which means that you only need to see something for three seconds in order for you to be aware of it, and then you lose your memory of it.

The second one is the short-term memory, which lasts around ten seconds. This tiny movement between the ultra short-term memory and the short-term memory takes between ten and thirteen seconds, and in Time Therapy we call this *now* the *fore-future*.

The third form is what we know as long-term memory, which in Time Therapy we refer to as the *unconscious*. So the fore-future *now* is a pulsation of ten to thirteen seconds.

You can even see this when observing the rate at which your eyelids blink. Effectively you are "blind" while you are blinking, but your brain fills the gaps through the processes of memory, so, for example, if you are driving a car you can still "see" while your eyes are closed. The so-called now is that tiny movement of the brain filling up the space in between the past and the future.

So whatever you remember is always influenced by the state that you are in at that moment. In Time Therapy we focus on what we call the fore-future, which describes the tiny movement forward toward something.

The fore-future

A simple example is a CD with six songs on it. Let's say that the first three songs have already been played, and that represents the past. The fourth song is about to be played, while the fifth and sixth songs have yet to be played, and these represent the future. The fourth song about to begin playing happens only because of just a little movement forward, which is not all the way to the fifth song nor all the way to the sixth song but just a little forward of the third, so that you are in the illusion of the now. This now is in fact the fore-future. It is difficult to grasp this concept with the cognitive mind. The illusion of the now is there simply because your brain is able to give you a sense of continuity.

It is exactly in this fore-future that the process of remembering occurs. Even if there are gaps in your memory, these gaps will be filled. The brain will produce stories in order to create a sense of security. We are constantly creating and telling stories in order to give ourselves a sense of security because the brain simply cannot function without security. The brain cannot deal with emptiness. It needs objects. The brain is attached to a constant need to be describing some event or object. This means that even the I breaks down time in order to give you the feeling of having some continuity of the I that in fact does not really exist.

One of the greatest mystics and founder of Indian classical yoga, Patanjali, spoke of one of the deepest truths when he said, "When there is one mind, when there is only one thought, then at this moment the past and the now are the same. When there is awareness without words the past and the now melt into each other." He did not say, "the past, the now and the future become one." He said, "The past and the now will be the same." When the now, which is constantly influencing it, and the past are the same, there is simply this tiny movement forward, into what we call the fore-future.

This is different from the huge step into the future that usually manifests as a desire. A preoccupation with the future elicits fear. The fore-future is not a thinking process; it has to do with being aware and therefore does not elicit fear. It is also about not clinging to the past, which creates a false structure of cause and effect.

Patanjali said, "When the one mind, the one thought is present, the past and the now are the same." He goes on to say that at exactly this moment, even the mind realizes that the concept of time, which embraces the past and future, is on one and the same level, while the qualities operate from a completely different level. He says, "Yoga is the art of seeing that as long as you are structured in time (and remember that when you analyze your past you are constantly structured in time), your qualities can never be activated."

The qualities, or your potential, can be active only once you begin to operate within the fore-future. This can only happen when you are not playing the illusionary game of being in the now. There is always a tiny movement from the past to the future, and as Patanjali taught, the past and the so-called tiny window to the future have to melt together.

The future causes your problems
It is fairly easy to understand how all actions are future oriented. You can never base your actions in trying to undo the past. What is meant by karma is that all actions that are oriented toward the future will have an influence on your life. Therefore, the past is not the cause of your problems; it is the future that is the cause.

If we do not train the mind and the thought processes to see things in this way, we are then not only never free of our own karma, we will simply not be able to work with energy. We will not be able to create transformation in our lives. We may – figuratively speaking – rearrange our psychological furniture, but essentially things do not change very much. It is still the same I or ego, only slightly rearranged. You may seem to have changed, but it will take up much of your time and energy to control yourself so as not to become aggressive or depressed, for example. If we know on a mental level that we should not be violent or judgmental toward someone and try our best to be loving and kind, we are then simply dealing with effort and not with transformation. The *should* is simply a moralistic standpoint.

Future-oriented actions

Our freedom is blocked by all the images we create of ourselves, not just because of the desire for power (although even this is questionable) but through all the moral structures and ideas about how we *should* be. All the shoulds can never encompass the whole of reality.

The mind cannot make a distinction between reality and illusion. You can create a moral structure that says "I should be more understanding," "I should be listening," "I should be more compassionate," but all of this requires an effort. Whenever anything incurs effort, you immediately invoke the risk of failing, which in turn produces guilt.

At least 60 percent of your energy is tied up in maintaining or observing that your behavior lives up to how you think you should be. Your meridians become blocked; the chakras, or energy centers, cannot function healthily; and there is little capacity to reach your potential, for you to be in your qualities. If the future represents fear and if the future is the cause of your problems, how then can you deal with fear, the future, if you do not make all your energy available for this? How can you deal with the unknown, which is such a large part of the cause of fear?

Dealing with the unknown

A body that is dealing with fear of the future cannot be relaxed in meditation, which is why many people find meditation difficult to enjoy, although it is widely recommended as a way to inner peace.

A body that is ready to deal with the unknown needs total vitality and real relaxation, which is very different from the temporary relaxation we find in some of the complementary therapies available. Real relaxation is when your body is totally awake because the body is the mirror of consciousness, and when you are totally awake in your mind, the body follows. It is a balance that occurs when the body is neither overly tense nor completely relaxed. It then has all the energy it needs to deal with the unknown. How can we reach a state of real relaxation?

It may seem that the answer to our problems lies in the future, in trying a new spiritual path, another kind of alternative therapy or even in the Christian idea of heaven or the kingdom of God. Yet our preoccupation with the future is actually creating our problems. We need to recognize that the past, our history, is only partially responsible for how we are now and that perhaps we can begin to explore our strengths and weaknesses in a different way.

Perhaps we can begin to change our perspective a little by looking first at how we create some of the emotional patterns in our lives.

CHAPTER 3

The Process of Feeling Patterns

Most of us like to think we are in some way different from other people. In the process of constructing our very own ego or sense of self, we have accepted the myth of our separateness, or individuality, as the basis of society in the West.

When we are caught up in our problems, we might feel so sorry for ourselves that we believe no one understands us or that we don't deserve to suffer so much. Statements like these are part of our feeling patterns, or how we respond in different situations and in relationship to others. However, our personal feeling patterns are not unique to us, even though they begin in our childhood and, like seeds planted in the ground of our mind, may or may not grow into problems as we become adults. All childhood feeling patterns belong to the realm of the basic nature of human beings. We each respond differently depending on the conditions and conditioning of our lives and how open or closed we are toward the future as an unknown.

As we have seen, looking into the past to try and understand why you feel jealous, for example, changes very little. What we need to do is to start an inquiry into the process of our jealousy, our anger, our envy or whatever is preventing us from working with our potential. Feeling

I don't agree.
Why often leads
to How.

Asking why is the process of understanding

patterns can create a dominant influence throughout childhood but can be resolved only by asking how, not why. To understand the dynamics of this process, we need to recognize that we all carry these feeling patterns in us irrespective of our personal history and that each person will react differently in the same situation. We need to understand that we are all the same in the sense that we are all made of the same substance and are subjected to the same laws.

Good and evil

According to Patanjali, one of the biggest mistakes and misunderstandings we make is in believing that good and bad are fundamental in shaping human nature, in causing us to behave in certain ways. The idea that when you are good or bad you create something that influences the whole of who you are, says Patanjali, is misguided. As good and bad are structured in time, they cannot be the cause of who you are.

This is a little difficult to understand, because the mind says, "Hang on a minute, if I am doing good, is it not creating a positive effect and if I am doing bad, is it not creating something negative?" The mind immediately creates a split between good and bad, then launches a "witch hunt" into what might be bad within you in order to be rid of it and to become a better person. This creates conflict and tension because what you end up with is a mind that is in theory in opposition to parts of itself. If it believes itself to be good, it begins to build up an image of being unique, of having special powers or gifts. It may even go so far as to believe that with self-mastery it will then be ready to help others, and this may be nothing more than a display of arrogance disguised as the duty of a "good" person. *Yes! Martars!*

Dualistic thinking

The teachings of Patanjali encourage us to stop for a second to consider this dilemma. In subscribing to the dualistic structure of good and bad, weaknesses and strengths, right and wrong, you are structuring yourself in time, and you will therefore always be in confusion and conflict. This is logical, although difficult for our conditioned minds to understand. If you feel aggressive and spend a large part of your life trying not to be aggressive, you will end up being aggressive toward yourself. Not only will you try to repress your aggression; at the same time you will create within the mind the concept of opposition, either aggression or nonaggression. *So? Where's your answer?!*

Patanjali claims that it is exactly this creating of opposition, which is the movement of duality, that creates the problem in the first place. Whenever one concept is replaced with an opposite concept, it is still exactly the same coin only turned over, while the coin as a whole remains the same. This reminds me of one of the most intelligent remarks made by J. F. Kennedy. In an interview, he was asked how he would proceed in his dialogue with the Russians to try to reduce the threat of a nuclear war. What size of reduction in missiles would he need the Russians to agree to in order to secure peace? He replied that merely reducing the arsenal of each side could never ensure peace.

To give another example, imagine two men standing on an oil tanker. Each one is armed with twenty matches and they are discussing how many matches they should throw away in order to be free of any threat of fire. As one match is enough to blow the whole thing up, to argue over whether only ten or fifteen should be thrown away is absurd. This is exactly the same as debating with yourself over which bits of yourself you should change. *Making peace with oneself*

In order to bring about real change we need to act as Patanjali says, so that the past and the now fuse into the fore-future. Here there is no need to change things around a little cosmetically. The question of who is bad and who is good is irrelevant. There are people out there who no doubt want to harm others, and the question of how they came to be as they are is not the point in this context. We know simply that harmful action exists.

Time and consciousness

The question is, does Patanjali mean that you should not judge someone for killing, or is he talking about something on a deeper level? Is he
saying that if you are constantly bad toward yourself, do not be surprised if, in time, there can only be aggression left? Is he saying that if
you think your weaknesses are the cause of your problems, then do not
be surprised when you find that you have nothing other than misery?

If we look for the cause of our misery, the chances are we will blame
our weaknesses. We will see the past as the cause of what is going on in
the fore-future. We tend to split our history and our future into two
separate phases, divided by an illusion of the now. As Patanjali says,
doing this only shows how we misunderstand the concepts of time and
consciousness.

From a biological standpoint, the past can only be recalled through a
memory. Memory, however, is not reliable. A huge amount of research
has been carried out that shows that memory never captures all of what
really has happened in the past. Part of the brain's function is to fill in
all the gaps in order that it may have a "logical conclusion." Whenever
you try to remember an incident from the past, the brain reacts as if
the incident is actually taking place. The brain does not distinguish
between memories and real events.

For example, say that you recall an unpleasant experience. In the moment of remembering it, as the brain cannot make the distinction
between reality and illusion, the brain behaves as if the unpleasant experience is happening now, and it immediately creates tension in your
body, activating various levels in your hormonal system.
Psychoimmunology has shown that this reduces your body's immune
system because your mind assumes that it is happening now and creates stress, alertness, fear and protection. This means that your brain
uses a huge amount of energy attempting to solve a problem that it
cannot solve, because it is not actually happening now. It is just a
memory. The physiological brain does not have the concept of past

and future; only the mind has that. This means that if you spend a lot of time trying to remember unpleasant things from your past – for example, your relationship with your mother, which seems to explain why you might have a problem with jealousy in current relationships – you create even more misery because your energy becomes absorbed in trying to solve the problems associated with that memory. If you continue to work on all of this, you are giving the brain the information that the problem is not solved. The brain continues to react to all of it as if the problems were happening at that very moment. This creates constant tension in the body and stress on the mental level.

Abhhaa) *I get it)*

Memory and intelligence

If the brain functions in this way, then it is fairly easy to see how working with your weaknesses cannot solve the problem and only increases the pressure on you to deal with it. It is easy to see how pointless it is to constantly focus on your past and the negative aspects of yourself instead of on your potential and qualities. Patanjali said that only when you stop dealing with consciousness at the level of time can the qualities have a chance to flower and unfold. When you are constantly focusing on the past and on negativity, you are in a constant state of alertness, tension and resistance. If you are in therapy, for example, and feeling resistant to delving into your past, this is not a reflection of your failure to confront your unpleasant memories; it is there because if you are constantly working negatively with your past, resistance is the natural outcome of the brain trying to solve something that cannot be solved.

thus, acceptance.

This is encapsulated in Plato's beautiful image of the cave, the light and the prisoners. Imagine people living in an underground cave since the day they were born. They are prisoners, sitting on the ground against the cave entrance. Their hands, feet and even their necks are tied so that they cannot turn and see anything but the inner wall of the cave in front of them. Behind them there is another high wall separating them from other people, their guards, who come and go, raising different objects of different shapes above the wall.

the serenity prayer!

Thanks to a fire burning behind the prisoners, trembling shadows are created on the wall that they are looking at. As this is the only experience they have in their lives, they believe that the shadows are the only things that exist in the world.

If we now imagine that one of them manages to escape and get out of the cave, we can be sure that first of all the sunlight will blind him for a while. Then he will get accustomed to it and will start discovering real shapes, colors, plants and animals, the clear lines of things, of which so far he only knew vague shadows. He will realize that the sun is actually the source of life and how the cave fire created the shadows in his prison. He will be able to run free in nature and think of the contrast with the life of his fellow prisoners still in the cave.

If he decides to go back to them and try to describe what he discovered, or to explain that the shadows they are looking at are only the imitation of reality, nobody will believe him. If he insists in trying to persuade them, they will get angry. They will be unable to accept that the only familiar thing in their lives – the shadows – is a deceit, an illusion. In the end they would kill him in order to maintain their peace of mind.

This image comes up again in the beautiful story of Don Quixote fighting windmills and in the beautiful Hindu saying "beware of maya" or illusion. The mind has to be present for the body and your biological consciousness to function. Maya is the brain trying to solve problems that are not actually there, so it simply loses all its energy and vitality and cannot function intelligently. It starts to fall out of rhythm. That is why music, which is rhythm, is very important in helping the brain to recharge its batteries. The brain needs to be a hologram, a oneness, and music helps it to reachieve that.

The definition of what we are comes out of knowledge, memory and the past. How can a brain be alive and intelligent when it is constantly dealing with the past? Patanjali says it cannot. Negative thinking and clinging to knowledge creates dullness in the mind. Intelligence is the movement of always being totally ready for what is new. Belief is the process of clinging to something and projecting, and what you are clinging to is in the future. Trust is the process of being ready to leave everything open. Faith is the process of no longer clinging to the mind so that there can then be true intelligence, a state of being able to see things clearly as they really are without clinging to old feeling patterns from the past.

Mind and body memory

Because the brain cannot distinguish between memory and real events, when you remember an unpleasant experience the body immediately becomes tense, and psychosomatic symptoms begin to arise. The connection between mind and body means that illness can sometimes be triggered by memory. The psychosomatic process is a result of the brain being confused about how to solve a problem that won't go away, and it eventually finds a physiological answer to the problem. While the brain feels it cannot solve the problem, it has no way of moving into the future. You are therefore trapped in wondering why there is no change despite having understood your problems.

What is happening here is that despite an intellectual understanding of the problem, your feelings remain the same; they are unchanged, and because of this the feelings then restart the whole process of having to reanalyze your situation and to understand why you are the way you are.

The brain and the mind

I am deeply convinced that in a hundred years from now, every illness will be treated by understanding the brain. Every illness can somehow be related back to the brain, not the mind. To believe that the brain and the mind are the same is a total misunderstanding. The process of thought – which is the mind – relates to just 10 percent of the total capacity of the brain. Most of the capacity of the brain is taken up with directing the physiology of the body. Without this direction, the organs of the body would not function. We need to work with the brain as well as with the emotions, and we need to learn how to use our thinking processes.

We are only just beginning to understand what is actually happening within the brain, how its dynamics work and how it might contribute to our well-being. We are beginning to see, for example, that all depressed people have a different amount of activity in their left and right cortices. We can see how the different combination of the various brain levels, and how they communicate with each other, has a tremendous impact on how we feel. Whatever we remember has an influence on our brain, and this can be dangerous if we are replaying negative thoughts or memories on a daily basis.

Forgetting and depersonalization

The most important thing therefore that the brain has to learn to do is to forget, but the mind puts up a strong resistance to this. There is a growing amount of research and study into the brain and dreams, and we are beginning to realize that dreams are probably only a mechanism whereby the brain can eliminate a memory that is no longer needed and that is merely taking up space. A healthy brain needs space just as a healthy relationship does.

On the psychospiritual level, forgetting is about forgiving. As we have seen, the moment you move energy toward the past, you are moving it toward something that no longer exists, and you create a diversion or blockage of your energy system. The energy needed to observe how you are at the present point in time, without any history, is no longer available. Instead of looking at your aggression, for example, from a historical perspective from which you can do nothing other than re-create aggression over and over again, try to look at it for what it is. The future is creating the past. It is this constant observation toward the unknown that determines how the past is going to look.

One of the fundamental laws of Christianity is the process of forgiveness. Forgiveness is the process of leaving the past absolutely and totally behind you. It is therefore the movement of dying from one moment to the next. In the teachings of Buddhism and the Tao, the practice of letting go or dying while living is considered to be essential for health. Often the mind, however, simply cannot deal with this, especially in people living with unresolved trauma.

Trauma

Traumatic experiences include single incidents like car crashes, mugging, rape, surgery or serious falls; sustained incidents over a period of time, for example, in domestic violence, war and abuse; or different incidents over a period of time. It is important to understand the difference between difficult experiences (such as not being loved as much as you would like to have been) and the experience of trauma.

In the case of trauma a person is often left feeling as if they have no perspective; they often feel as if their life has been completely shattered, and they are unable to function any longer. Their recovery depends to a large extent on the conditions of their life – for example, whether they live alone or with others – if they have a supportive network of friends, if they have love in their lives, this can make a crucial difference to their capacity to heal.

Children have a tremendous amount of healing force within them. This healing force only breaks down when they are left feeling as if there were no perspective. For example, if a woman is raped or a child is constantly abused, then as a result of that the woman or the child can lose their perspective, and so their system breaks down. The rest of us may have had experiences that have been unpleasant, hurtful and even dreadful, but the capacity for self-healing, which is always present, can heal us emotionally as well as on a biological level. Illness happens when there is no longer any perspective because the mind simply cannot deal with emptiness or nothing.

Healing and perspective

When a person's sense of perspective breaks down, there are significant energy changes, for example, depression. You can tell a depressed person that you love and care for them as much as you want but it will not help lift them out of their state. This is because the depressed person needs to rediscover their own perspective in order that they may function healthily again, and depressed people often need to begin to express love in order to recover.

So the difference between illness and health is a question of how much perspective there is. A placebo shows clearly the power that perspective has in defining the future. The effect of a placebo is that a person may start to believe in something again, and it works because it offers them a perspective. Illness always has something to do with a loss of perspective. The movement from illness to normality is only the first step in becoming healthy. Most of us can function in everyday life, but we don't feel really healthy.

The first step in helping the mind to function better is to have a perspective, and the second step from what we think of as normality to health, or even to enlightenment (whatever that may mean), is to be able to step out of the perspective into that which is beyond the past with all its history, all its conditions. This is what wisdom, enlightenment and mysticism are all about. This is what we mean when we talk about a psychospiritual approach to health and healing, and this is where the qualities come into play in returning us to true health and wellbeing. In the process, the mind learns not to avoid what we think of as emptiness, insecurity and the unknown, but it also discovers how to deal with the unknown.

The unknown and depersonalization

The first thing we need to do is to take our attention away from any personal structure to be able to observe fully. This is because attaching to personal structures always requires that we go into the past, which, as we have seen, disperses and slows down our energy. If we want to work with our aggression, for example, can we simply observe what happens when we become aggressive without needing to find an explanation for our behavior? In other words, can the mind take it away from the personal level?

If you can just observe your emotions as they arise on an impersonal level, without interpreting anything, then two things will occur. You no longer ask the question "why am I aggressive," but instead you will find yourself looking at how aggression manifests, how it moves through you, how the process of it unfolds. Instead of asking yourself why the aggression is there, you will suddenly find yourself out of *center-space-time*. At this point you will find yourself connected with your true potential or your qualities. We all have a quality aura, or soul consciousness – our potential and our future. How can we use it to work with feeling patterns, like aggression, that are always based on fear?

Changing our feeling patterns

In scientific terms, we all have a magnetic field around us that is much more than our personal structure. You could not exist without the quality aura, as the main structure of body-mind relies on the existence of the quality aura in order to come into being, or to be born. When this is contacted through simple awareness or depersonalization, we stop seeing our weaknesses as personal or belonging to us, and we can begin to create the energy of change.

How can we learn to forget and so leave behind the pattern of accumulating more and more of the past, therefore creating an enormous conflict within the brain? In order to do this we need to understand the three conditioning behaviors of evolution. Every brain functions in the same way, although not every brain has exactly the same structure.

So if we choose not to give it a history or a personal structure, this is the process of depersonalization through which we are immediately connected with the qualities, which represent our potential. Potentials relate to the future. Within every individual this potential is much more important than the inside structure of center-space-time, which has to do with the I or the ego. Even if you believe in reincarnation, it becomes nonsensical to deal with the I. You must instead deal with that which is not going to die – the quality aura. If you look at aggression without giving it a personal structure, you observe the movement of aggression without raising the question of why it is present. It then becomes possible to see that the process of the feeling pattern of aggression is essentially energy structured on the basis of fear, and fear is always structured in the future, never in the past. Depersonalization does not mean that there is no feeling with it. The feeling is very much there, but the mind does not create a history or personalized structure.

CHAPTER 4

The Dynamics of Thought

Resistance and energy

When we resist a feeling, the resistance creates an atmosphere of sadness in our consciousness as a response to the feeling being repressed. It is the sadness that we reexperience later in association with our resistance and not the repressed feeling. The more we resist our feelings, the more sadness we accumulate. Where there is no longer any resistance to feelings, through the process of desireless awareness, the sadness soon disappears naturally. Sadness itself becomes a medium for transformation. It is only when sadness is personalized as self-pity that blockages occur. If we can go fully into the feeling of sadness, surrender to it and set it free, we promote a flow in energy. Freely flowing energy is experienced as a feeling of love or compassion. This is energy in movement without resistance.

As we know only too well, this is not how we usually deal with our feelings. If we remember the example of the girl with the quality of shyness, imagine her sitting at home trying to understand and analyze her shyness and feeling some self-pity about her situation. Her shyness makes it difficult for her to mix with other people, to go to a bar or to a disco, and in the long run it will somehow even have an influence on her ability to have a relationship. She does not realize that because she is focusing so much on the problem, she has no energy left to just feel curious, to go out and discover whether or not it is possible for something to happen despite her shyness. Her brain is totally pre-occupied with the idea that she has to solve the problem of her shyness before being able to do anything else. This in turn blocks her energy in mind and body. When she does go out, she has very little energy left to become involved in anything or to try something new. Instead of focusing so much on the problem, as we have seen, what she really needs to do is to forget about her shyness and forgive herself for being shy, in order to bring about a change in her situation. This can only be done on a psychospiritual level, by moving away from herself and her attempts to understand, away from the brain-consciousness that is focused on her weakness and on trying to find a solution.

Liberating the brain

When we understand something, it involves our biological and biopsychological consciousness. We can understand why a car has broken down and fix it, why we need to buy a ticket before travelling on a plane, but we cannot understand love. On the psychospiritual level, understanding stops.

If we look at this statement in terms of concepts, for example, aggression versus nonaggression, this leads us to the concept of shoulds, which as we have seen simply does not change anything. If we say to ourselves, "I will let go of my feelings of aggression," the mind becomes fixed on trying to let go. You cannot command yourself to forget, as it is not something you can bring about by using your brain in the usual way. The question is how can you forget, how can you liberate the brain from the blockage in its energy so that it can flow, so that it can vibrate, so that it can become a hologram again, so that the different brain waves do not collapse into each other?

Look at how relaxed the brain becomes when we listen to music if we do not try to understand the music. If we try to understand the music, the brain gets into a terrible pickle again because understanding includes memory, knowledge and experience. Curiosity and learning, on the other hand, involve a moving away from oneself, which creates space for the brain. Your qualities always have the possibility to manifest only when you move away from yourself. Imagine you are holding a torch as near as possible toward you and facing you. How much light would there be? Then watch what happens when you move the torch away from you. The more you move it away from you, the more light you create.

Similarly, the movement of thoughts, the brain, feeling, the whole secret of how to forget and to create a transformation lies in moving the light or the torch of awareness away from you into space. Out of this comes a form of "direct seeing." How successfully we can transform our lives by moving away, creating space and seeing things as they really are depends very much on our perspective. In order to see how this works, it is important to explore our thought processes.

Thought structures

There are three types of thought structures and two different thought processes. To work on the level of consciousness, we need to be able to distinguish between the different "flowers of consciousness," or thoughts.

The first thought structure has to do with the ability to move in time between the past and the future. This is quite easy to see, as we spend 70 percent of the day in thought structure one, moving with the help of our memories into the past. The past and the memory of it may be close to reality, but a lot of what is associated with it is invention. In the first thought structure you may also move into the future, and it is absolutely possible to see what you feel is the future. There is an African tribe that says "the past is before me and the future is behind me" because I can see the past very clearly, but the future I can see less well, and therefore it is behind me.

You can tune into a part of the future, but this is usually only as good as weather forecasting. So the movement toward the future includes even more illusion than the movement toward the past. Many people are fascinated by past-life memory, but we are beginning to realise that it is largely an invention. It is not that past lives do not exist, but if you are in a state of relaxation and you suddenly get pictures of having been, for example, Socrates, it is very unlikely that you were Socrates himself but simply that you have tuned into that vibration of consciousness. Consciousness is not limited to you; it is never personal. Just think about this for a moment. We spend 70 percent of the day in thought structure one, moving between the past and the future. This is neither good nor bad; they are just processes.

Thought structure two is more difficult to observe. Remember that thought is always a description. If you take away thought structure one, which is the movement between the past and the future, you are in what some people call the now, but the now does not really exist; it is an illusion. Thought structure two is one of judging, comparing and explaining.

When we are sitting in the so-called now, we have left behind the past and future, and we immediately have thoughts such as "am I sitting correctly?," "do I understand what is going on?" or "is it going to be over soon?" Here you find a constant commentary on what is happening. We spend 29 percent of time in thought structure two. It is possible to see the difference between these two thought structures within the aura system. Thought structure one will show in the mental aura as a movement with quite a slow vibration. Thought structure two has a faster vibration (faster does not mean better, just different). Most of us spend our whole lives in thought structures one and two. In thought structure two, we are constantly judging ourselves and conditioning ourselves with negative attitudes. We believe that if we can understand why we are thinking negatively or what the connection is between our present pattern of behavior and our past (which again means having to activate thought structure one), we will then solve our problem. All that happens is the equivalent of trying to transform a room by rearranging the furniture. What then is thought structure three?

Into the fore-future

In comparison with thought structures one and two, thought structure three does not by definition take you from one point in time to another. It is not a clear description of anything. Thought structure three, where we reside 1 percent of our time, is what we call the movement toward something, or the movement into the fore-future. There is no now. There is a past, the future and the fore-future.

Let us take the simple example of love. You cannot really fully describe love even if you use a thousand descriptions. Love is a constant movement toward something without seeing or knowing exactly where the movement is going. Compassion is a constant movement without having a goal, a desire, a fulfillment or a description. Thought structure three, which is a flower of consciousness, is exactly this movement that you can be aware of, but it cannot be given a clear identification, conclusion or interpretation.

Whenever you have the feeling of just being there, in the so-called now, as in meditation, you are in thought structure three. If your brain waves were measured while in this thought structure, you would see more gaps between the periods of brain activity.

In these gaps in the usual activity of our brain, the fore-future is the nearest time structure where our qualities become manifest. Every potential, every quality is alive because of the activation of thought structure three, which is a movement toward the fore-future. If the mind can begin to observe not only the distinction between the various descriptions but also begin to recognize the presence of qualities, it can begin to function differently. If it can also begin to see the subtle differences between thoughts, as in thought structure one, two and three, we can begin to see ourselves and others in a completely different way. The mind will then be able to understand the two thought processes with ease.

Thought processes

The associative thought process is always connected with thought structures one and two. It involves the constant association between things and is used by all of us 70 percent of the time. It is the most powerful tool at our disposal for evoking the past. If we reinterpret the words of the Buddha, for example, then the way to happiness can occur only when the associative thought process is inactive or absent, as this is how we constantly create our own suffering – by association.

The associative thought process has the ability to create meaning even where there is none in reality: we postpone living this life by thinking about what will happen in the next life, or we believe that when we start to behave differently, or when we grow up or when our chakras function better, then we can start to really live. If you are honest and you cut through the associative thought process, you will realize that most of this is nonsense. Love does not have conditions, and this in its deepest sense means that it needs no prerequisite before it can manifest. On the other hand, having a healthy body does matter, as it will have an influence on the degree to which the quality aura is able to manifest. The aura is the outcome of the magnetic resonance of the cells within the body. Love belongs to that part of the energy body beyond the aura structure. The worst excuse that any of us can make is to claim that we cannot love because parts of ourselves are not functioning properly, or that we need more preparation to first attain certain levels of consciousness. This is the greatest misuse of the associative process – it means putting off being in touch with the world and realizing that no one is different from anyone else. Our histories may be different, and this is what defines our individuality.

The associative thought process is also constantly creating pictures. If pictures were not associated with thoughts, you would not be able to imagine the picture. Whatever you see inside your mind makes you immediately create a description of it, and you therefore become aware of it. Taking sound as an example, we become aware of a sound only when it registers in the brain in the form of a pattern. For example, if I use the Swahili word *arda*, you may create an association to the sound of that word. However, when I say *green*, you immediately know what I mean. You may not be aware of the picture you have of *green*, but it is there in your brain, otherwise you would not know what I mean by the word. However, turning it the other way round, when you look at the color green, you immediately have the word for it even though you may not be aware of having it. Otherwise you would not be able to recognize the color.

This is exactly how the whole dream structure works. You have a dream that is first in picture form, and only later on do you describe it in words in order to explain it to someone else. Being able to explain the dream means that you have already created a description of it. You can then indulge in uncovering the symbolic meaning of the elements in the dream.

Thought and the senses

The senses cannot be separated from one another. Using the processes of seeing, sensing and listening, together with the use of words, we interact and relate to one another, so whatever is happening becomes more of a hologram, or a whole. Images, accompanied by a description, form the first steps to consciousness. While you are listening, at the same time you are creating descriptions. If this did not happen, then you just would not be able to hear.

For example, if you move from the countryside into a flat located near a railway line that has a train passing by every ten minutes, initially you will hear the noise of each train that passes. Immediately you describe what the noise is. Once you become accustomed to the noise of the train, you will stop giving it a description. If you are asked if it is not very noisy living so close to passing trains, you will claim not to hear the trains anymore; you have stopped listening.

Most of us are very attentive when it comes to knowledge, when we think we need to have knowledge in order to pass examinations or to maintain our position within society. But are we really listening when it comes to how our brain works and what thinking consists of? Do we really try to find out what thinking is? Not what we think, but what the process of thinking is? We do not because we think we already know everything there is to know about thinking, as we do it all day long. In the same way as we cut out the noise of the train, we cut the description, which means that we have reduced our awareness.

This state of mind is what Gurdjieff called being "fast asleep," and in his work he tried to wake us up to how easy it can be to go through life being unaware of how we relate to ourselves and to others. Whenever we create habits within a relationship, it becomes miserable and will start to fall apart. Sooner or later the relationship will end because we stop listening to each other. We go into the associative thought process and fail to hear the space in between. If we believe we know everything about something or someone, we fail to really listen and see what is happening; we never create any space.

The brain not only has the ability for curiosity, learning and decision making, but it also has a proportionate amount of ability to forget. If you look back on your life realistically and globally, you will find that from birth until your midtwenties you were probably in more misery than you would like to admit. Your body and your mind were struggling to become an adult, to understand the world you lived in and to engage in work.

You may have had to deal with lack of success, failures in love, separations and losses, as well as all the physiological changes taking place in the body. It takes twenty-eight years for the mental aura to develop completely. In the first sixteen to seventeen years we are mostly imprisoned in the processes of learning, taking examinations, struggling just to stay afloat materially, having misunderstandings. But how much of this do we actually remember? Not very much, and this is because the brain has the intelligence to allow those memories to fade, recognizing that this is all over and done with.

If the past really played a major role in determining who we are now, many of us would be paralyzed into nonaction. Yet we are still moving forward with the help of our brain. Despite all the negativity, beauty is still showing. How often have you been against yourself, how often have you criticized yourself, how often have you thought yourself not worth it, how often have you not loved and still your inner beauty remains unaltered? None of this stops you from being creative, or loving, and your body remains strong despite the stresses of those first twenty-odd years. If anything, it has become even more awake. Yes, there may be some weaknesses and some problems, but this is not entirely the result of what has happened to you.

Forgiveness and freedom

If we focus on a situation to do with someone in the past and our brain is constantly seeking revenge, this is not harming the person in question; it is doing tremendous harm only to itself. For example, if you feel that your mother is largely responsible for who you are now and should be made to see this, it will not alter anything within your mother. You may only succeed in creating guilt within her, dissipating your energy and maybe creating more problems for yourself. If, instead of helping your mother to free herself, you take revenge by blaming her and causing guilt within her, do not be surprised if you then end up feeling guilty yourself. You are not going to be different as a result of your mother admitting that she did not take as much care of you as she should have. Blaming simply creates more of the energy of guilt and therefore more blockages and diversions.

Freedom will not come to you by knocking at the door to love and waiting for someone else to open it. Freedom comes when you open the door. In fact, there is really no locked door. You may believe that your mother closed the door, but she was not able to lock it and throw away the key. Your mind and your qualities are independent of the actions of others.

You may in the course of your life experience suffering, but you always have the possibility of stepping out of it again. People who were in concentration camps will tell you that the only way not to end up being totally fearful, the only way to live a constructive life afterward is through the act of forgiveness. Seeing forgiveness as it really is does not mean giving it any moral value; it allows you to see forgiveness as the movement of leaving the past behind. It is in the very nature of the brain to forget the past and to move on.

The creative brain

Once we realize that the whole brain (including the 10 percent that is the mind) is a a creative process, then our attitude toward the brain changes. We are suddenly aware of the creative process and do not just accept that whatever is there is meant to be there. We can begin to create a relationship to the brain and to the whole movement of thought. If we have an influence on what goes on in our brain, we can become the master of our own mind.

This is what the mystics meant when they taught us to have control over our thoughts. It is not achieved by repressing what we do not like and judging what goes on in our mind. It does not involve repressing the past and thoughts of the future – which by the way can only be done by using the processes of thought structure two or in trying to destroy the processes of thought structure one. It does not involve thought structure one trying to control thought structure two. All you have to do is to simply move to the motivative thought process. It is connected with thought structure three, which involves a movement toward the fore-future. The motivative thought process occurs when your actions are no longer just structured for your own good or born out of your particular moral philosophy. You simply realize that body/

mind/aura and thought structures one and two function beautifully but have nothing to do with spirituality.

Intuition

Intuition simply means that you are in a balance between listening, seeing and feeling words. Intuition is about not being in a habit of thinking that you know how the process of thinking works. Everyone has the ability to be intuitive, everyone has the third eye and everyone has the ability to see auras to a certain limited extent.

Being intuitive is not a question of whether or not you have these abilities; it has more to do with the question of how great your own inner boredom is. Boredom is habit, an absence of awareness, a lack of interest and openness. Arrogance also hinders intuition when you feel you know everything there is to know and so you fail to really listen and to see.

It is impossible to live in this world without the associative thought process, but we need to be aware of how thinking works in order to be intuitive. Once you start to be aware of the process of thought, you will always be aware of pictures, words, "fast" and "slow" feelings, of the different thought structures, the past, the future and the processes of judgment. Then you will be free. It is the I that brings with it the prison of nonfreedom. Nonfreedom does not come from your history. You were born to be free. Nonfreedom or imprisonment comes from within your mind. On the psychospiritual level, the associative thought process is a hindrance and a barrier to stillness because the opposite of stillness is not noise, it is fear.

The brain and desireless awareness

The question is whether you wish to use this beautiful brain with its 10 percent mind as a creative process. It is all about your brain, your mind and the creation of relationship. It is the constant movement of interdependence or mutuality, creativity in a relationship to everything, which is God, or in the words of the Buddha, the nature of Buddha-hood. It carries within it a tremendous ability to learn, to be curious, to make decisions, which means making choices, to remember and even more importantly to forget. It is thought that creates part of you because thought is the flowering of consciousness. Consciousness is what you are, and consciousness is more than your history.

Here you suddenly come to thought structure three, which is a tiny movement forward into the fore-future. It does not involve the future, as the future belongs to thought structure one and is goal-oriented, involving desire. Thought structure three is desireless awareness. It is a tiny movement toward no goal and is without any element of clinging. In the Buddha's words, it is the process of not being attached.

If there is no attachment to anything and no desire, and if human and universal forces are always in a movement, then there is no now. Instead there is awareness of a tiny movement forward into the fore-future. The movement into the fore-future has the element of detachment within its movement, which is why Jesus says, in one of his most beautiful sentences, "movement and stillness at the same time" (Thomas Evangelou). Jesus refers to us as visitors in this world, mere passers-by. Our nature he claims is a movement within stillness. It cannot be more beautifully put, that we are movement and stillness at the same time.

Current preoccupations with Jesus seem to reflect the associative thought process by focusing on the historical facts of how he lived and what he did. According to orthodox Christianity, we must care about the future and try to make sure we get to heaven. What Jesus really taught is that we don't have to care about the future; we can be like the flowers of the field, which do not need an agency, priest or religion to save them. Only then can we become truly religious, as religiousness is the sudden movement into the fore-future.

Thought structure three and transformation

On the psychospiritual level, memory no longer plays a pivotal role, as time becomes unimportant. No history is created here. In thought structure one, which is geared toward the future, we automatically create a past, a history. However, in thought structure three, we have the tiny movement forward in desireless awareness. Being in thought structure three always involves a movement; we can never stand still, as having no movement implies death. At this point where there is no accumulation of memory, there is constant transformation, and this is the art of dying.

To move either with thought structure one into the future or to cling to the past is a barrier to transformation. This in no way discounts the past but merely asks you to recognize the problems in identifying with it. Clinging to your history means that you place the responsibility for who you are and for what is happening to you elsewhere, and this takes away your freedom to choose. Clinging means that you identify with the past. Clinging means you identify and create an individual history with a cause and effect structure to it with all the attendant beliefs, explanations etc., which may provide some temporary relief from your problems but will not allow transformation to take place.

However, if what you want is transformation and enlightenment, as Patanjali says, move out of time and allow the past and the now to converge. To do this go into thought structure three and be in that tiny movement forward where there is no calculation as to why you are doing whatever it is that you are doing. Here you will find no goal or desire but only a movement. The Chinese master Lao Tsu called this movement of energy the "flow," which is in the word *Qi* as in qigong or *chi* as in tai chi.

Thinking about thinking

In working with these ideas we need to remember that we cannot observe our thinking processes or inquire into our thoughts by thinking about it all. In classical meditation we can just observe our thoughts, whatever arises in our mind, without attaching to it. Observing how thought actually works, however, is different from observing the contents of our mind. Thought is the main barrier to getting in touch with our potential, our qualities. We need to know about the different structures of thought – thought structures one, two and three – and our associative and motivative thought processes, but we also need to inquire further into how thought works.

CHAPTER 5

The Process of Thinking

Thought and the qualities

The quality aspect of the soul is the first thing that is born together with the already functioning body and brain. Gradually, over the first two years, thinking or thoughts are created. As we grow up, the more that thought is relied upon or the more developed the ability to think, the greater is the tendency for thought to repress or overshadow the qualities.

When we begin to examine thought and the process of thought, we need to try to do it without activating the process of thinking. This sounds difficult, but it will help to remember that thinking is a description of something and that the future without a perspective is fear. If we take the analogy of a painter and his painting, the future without perspective is when you are there in front of a blank sheet of paper, you have the paint ready and you do not know what to paint. When the future is present without any perspective, there is fear, and fear presents as thinking or thoughts.

A future with perspective, on the other hand, means that you are totally vitalized because you know what you want to paint; you just have to paint it. Here there is no fear, there is only action in nonaction, and you lose yourself in moving away from yourself. Moving away from yourself does not mean simply moving toward something else or another person; it means moving into the fore-future.

Thought dominates us all. Everything that has been created so far by human beings, from planes to wonderful paintings to this book, has been through the processes of thought. Most of us believe the brain is used for thinking, but, as we mentioned earlier, biologically 90 percent of the brain is directed toward the physiological care of the body, and only 10 percent of it is used for thinking.

Out-of-body consciousness and thought

The lack of expression of our qualities is not as a result of how well cared for or how loved we were as children. Even if we are loved, our qualities can still be overshadowed by thought. It is only through a deep, direct relationship in seeing or feeling what thinking is and how thinking works that we can have an influence on how the qualities can express and manifest in this life.

Is mind consciousness the same as thinking? It includes thinking, but when Descartes said, "I think therefore I am," it was more of a self-observation than an accurate conclusion. Someone who cannot express thought or has lost the part of the ability to think – for example, with Alzheimer's disease – is still conscious. If thought cannot be used to analyze or to observe thinking, how can we become aware of our thought processes?

Imagine white light being directed onto a large white sheet of paper on which you intend to paint a picture. At the beginning, you will see only a white sheet and a white light directed onto this sheet. After a few minutes, however, you will see a change. When white light hits white paper, the white light gets refracted into different colors. Imagine that this white light is consciousness or awareness, and whenever it is broken up, what we have are thoughts. If colors represent thoughts, all colors are present in white, but you need some interference in order to see them. The interference to awareness is provided by your brain.

The picture and the frame

Using the symbol of color to represent the descriptions produced by thought with white representing awareness, and a frame representing collections of ideas, we can see how thinking breaks consciousness into pieces. The break in consciousness is a natural consequence of thinking, and various thoughts are then put into frames – for example, religious ideologies are given names like Allah, God or Jehovah depending on our culture – so we can see how God then has a different meaning for different people.

To give another example, say you are looking at a tree. Either you create a relationship to it by simply watching the tree or you can start to frame it and describe it. All you need to know is that this is a tree and that you are able to distinguish it from a flower. The act of distinguishing one tree from another is like breaking up consciousness, and the framing or description comes in with thoughts like how old it is or whether it is an apple tree or a plum tree. To look without description is possible only when you can move away from mind consciousness to out-of-body consciousness. In the famous Zen master's saying, "When I point with my finger to the moon, do not mistake the finger for the moon." Don't mistake the frame for the whole picture.

Overshadowing the qualities

If you believe that your childhood is responsible for how you are now, this means that your internal thinking pattern has become more important than the reality of seeing what is in front of you. The faculty of thought has become more important than the true living experience, and it is exactly when this framing or description starts that the qualities begin to be overshadowed. Remember that the brain does not know the difference between reality and thought. Whether you think of a tree or you actually see the tree, the reaction within the brain is the same. If you are depressed or if you think very deeply about being depressed, then the brain will activate the same hormones in both circumstances. The brain does not make a distinction between "I am now in thinking mode" and "this is the reality of what is happening now." Therefore, both the experience of something fearful and simply the thought of the same thing can create within the brain the same reaction of psychological fear.

On the psychospiritual level as opposed to the biological level, there is no psychological fear that is independent of thought. In other words, all psychological fears are dependent or arise only because of thought. There is absolutely no future apart from that which is created by thought. The future is fear, and fear is thought. Problems occur as a result of framing or the description of the fear. This cannot be observed by thinking about it because you cannot inquire about thought through engaging in the act of thinking. Thoughts have become so dominant in our culture that very often we no longer have a direct perspective of how anyone really is, including ourselves. We even form relationships with other people by thinking about what they might be thinking and reacting to that, not by observing how they are. This helps us to get into relationships very quickly, but it creates a huge problem once you have structured a relationship based on thought.

In a relationship, if you are constantly thinking about what you think the other person thinks and therefore act accordingly, then you will see less and less of that person in their true sense. In the end, you will be totally confused about whether or not you love the person. How can you know if you love the person if you no longer see them for who they really are? How can you know how you feel about them if you have created only a thinking attitude and a thinking relationship to them? How can you know what you really want? If the brain cannot make the distinction between what is real and what is not, the moment you have created a thinking relationship with anything, even if it has no basis in reality, it will set up a reaction in the body.

Perception, thought and reality

A woman with bulimic symptoms (overeating and vomiting) goes to see a therapist. If the therapist relates to her from the point of view of a particular psychological belief system, the woman's condition will be seen as a result of something in her past. If the woman is also feeling increasingly depressed, the therapist might fail to realize that the depression is not because of what happened in the past but a simple biological reaction to being bulimic. If someone vomits all the time, they lose a lot of essential minerals, and this alone can make them depressed. Bulimia is a classic symptom of repressed and overshadowed qualities, a symptom of a rebellious quality, a desperate cry to find a way back to expressing one's qualities. In a case like this the first thing the woman needs is to get to a level of physical well-being where she will stop losing essential nutrients and to ease her depression and the headaches that commonly accompany this sort of physical state.

The way we perceive people is based on a picture we have of them, composed of our expectations, beliefs, prejudices and hopes. If the therapist uncovers the cause of the bulimia as being due to abuse by a parent, this alone will not solve the woman's problems. She may even tell the therapist that she thinks the bulimia stems from a recent car crash in which her friend died and not from abuse as a child.

The therapist may tell her the car accident must have been a catalyst or trigger for her loss of the father after he abused her. If she does not agree, the therapist may describe her as being resistant and repressed and may never actually look at the whole person, the complete picture, and will see only the frame created by this thinking process. Framing takes place when thinking is no longer used in an intelligent way. The frame always creates a prison. If we frame ourselves in this way, how can we really see ourselves?

Mistaken patterns of thinking

The cortex, which is the newest addition to the brain, is where consciousness is broken down into ideas and thoughts. Around one and a half to two years old, a child will be able to differentiate between a subject and an object, between her/him and others. This is when thought begins to be reflective and then follows a slow, gradual over-shadowing of qualities.

The mind is a beautiful instrument, but you can commit psychological suicide with it. Mistakes can be made by relying too much on thinking. One of the most common mistakes of this sort is the tendency to generalize by connecting a thought with a feeling to some general structure. For example, your wife does something that upsets you, and you generalize by saying, "You are always making stupid mistakes" instead of "This situation makes me upset and makes me see you as stupid." This is one of the worst thought processes encountered frequently within relationships and in the education system.

Another mistake that most of us tend to deal with slightly better is the habit of thinking in opposites, either this or that, black or white, pleasant or unpleasant. For example, in the associative thought process we can see how God is described as either vengeful or loving, helping or not helping, providing or taking away. In the motivative thought process we simply cannot do this; God is simply communication.

We also tend to be in habitual denial of reality; we fail to see things as they really are. We build up a belief system because we feel we cannot live without beliefs. Not only do we see everything from this point of view, but we also adjust everything to fit in with our belief system. We think in terms of either/or and then defend our particular beliefs, failing to see what is in front of us. If you have just won a million dollars in the lottery and you happen to walk by a rose bush in bloom, you will experience the roses as beautiful. If, on the other hand, you happened to be seriously depressed at the time, you may not even see the roses. Even if you were given a rose you would probably not find it at all beautiful while you were feeling depressed.

Negative thinking

Reality is colored by the associative thought process or description. This means that the rose cannot be in direct communication with you nor you with it because your thinking is structured around adjusting to what you believe at the time. Out of this comes one of the biggest misunderstandings that has been constructed – the fixation on that which is negative.

We have been programmed to believe that if you can get rid of or understand your negativity, then you will be a different person. By indulging in negative thinking we fall prey to the associative thought *or description* process. Negative thinking means that we are against our own being, and as long as there is description using the associative thought process rather than direct communication, there can be no real change, no transformation and no enlightenment.

You may think you have succeeded in getting rid of something that has been worrying you, but you will still feel that you lack something, which will make you feel less than whole. Or you may end up striving for perfection, thinking that this is what you need to do before you can start living. Thinking is the process of description, and description is the absence of stillness. Our problems themselves are not the obstacle; it is the constant need to describe, identify them and keep them ever more tightly bound to us, giving us no prospect of freedom, that is where our true suffering lies. This is what the Buddha meant when he said we need to let go of our attachments in order to be free. *let go of description*

We also use the associative thought process to create a mental picture of the future and include anything negative that might possibly happen – we "hope for the best, plan for the worst." If the brain cannot make a distinction between reality and unreality, we can see how this *this is our today's society thermostate – we are stuck there as a socidyl.* constant thinking about what could go wrong in the future creates tension, and activates the associative thought process even more. How can you be in communication with whatever is there, which is the motivative thought process, if you are constantly in fear? If you are constantly in fear you cannot communicate; you can only try to escape.

Another typical consequence of relying heavily on thinking is to take everything personally. For example, to believe that you are jealous as a result of the way your parents behaved toward you is a misunderstanding. Jealousy is a natural human response; if you reduce it to personality, you will never solve the problem of jealousy. The fear of the future and the idea that there is somewhere out there someone who loves someone else more than you also arise from relying too much on thinking.

Learning to think healthily

Can you see how thinking in this way can interfere with your being? The only way to ensure that overshadowing of your qualities does not become increasingly stronger until one is totally identified with thought is through an awareness of how to think differently. The more you identify with thought, the less you can be aware of consciousness.

In the process of thinking we need to become so aware that we can distinguish between intelligent thinking, which is the motivative thought process, and descriptive, analytic thinking, which is the associative thought process. A child does not say, "I am hungry" and then start the process of description, for example, "Maybe if I could have a banana now, how fantastic that would be because I am hungry...." It simply realizes it is hungry. We need to be aware of the constant description going on in our mind that takes us away from the initial motivating thought.

We need to be constantly attentive to our thoughts and in a relationship to them. We need to consciously observe our thoughts from a level that is not thought-oriented. Thought cannot analyze or observe itself; we can only see what is happening in our thoughts from the perspective of the observer who is observing the Timeless observer. For this we need to cultivate stillness.

Using the motivative thought process (which is always the first part of the thought process), it is possible to see that how we are now is a consequence of how we are thinking at this moment. It is possible for us to direct our own thoughts and take some control over our mind – control not in the usual sense, but as Krishna counselled Arjuna in the *Bhagavad-Gita*, to achieve control by being aware. By shifting to a new way of thinking with awareness, the shadow, which represses the qualities, moves or lightens naturally by itself without any effort.

- Know that you can understand and at the same time be aware of how your thought processes work.
- Use your motivative thinking process to be aware of the associative thinking process and so influence the attitude of your associative thinking.
- Use your motivative thinking process to always be aware of the inner dialogue, the description that is running constantly in your head.
- Be constantly aware of how you build up description in the associative thought process when you focus on wanting to be, for example, different, better, loved, more powerful, perfect or enlightened.
- Stop analyzing problems. Look at them directly, without asking why they exist. Inquire into how you might solve them and move into the fore-future, which is the motivative process.
- When you are searching for a solution to a problem, choose the most practical one. If you tend to go for the most difficult solution, this shows how your thinking is trapped in the descriptive process of wanting perfection. When you take a simple and practical approach, the associative thought process is not activated.
- Ask yourself if you are ready to examine your belief systems and if necessary let them go. Be careful before you say yes because 80 percent of the ego identifies with belief systems, theoretical structures, habits and rituals. For example, if you have developed the habit of praying to God in times of difficulty and found that it helps you, it will not be easy to stop. As the Zen master said: If you meet the Buddha on the road, kill him – in other words, attachment to any belief system is not the point; the point is to be free.

• Ask yourself if your motivative thinking process is ready to be open and free to engage in whatever is happening.

Thinking, acknowledgement and love

When the Buddha taught about suffering and how to end it, he spoke about how we need to acknowledge what is happening and to let it be. We often find this teaching difficult to understand; in the face of injustice and violence, especially toward children, how can we just let things be? However, he did not mean that if there is injustice we should just accept it. It is important to recognize the difference between *acceptance* and *acknowledgement* of something.

Acceptance implies making an effort despite our real feelings about something, whereas to acknowledge means that we see it for what it is. We can acknowledge something on the thinking level without having to accept it; for example, if a close friend commits suicide, we need to be able to express our grief and acknowledge what has happened instead of focusing on analyzing exactly why she did it. If we are urged to accept her death and get over it as quickly as possible, we might try to block out our grief in order to make others feel better.

Similarly, tolerance suggests that we do not agree with something, but we have to for some reason. Acceptance and tolerance both imply that we are really against something, but because we have no possibility of changing it we accept it, and we may spend years going over it in our minds or even becoming bitter about how we may have compromised ourselves in accepting the situation. If we acknowledge it, however, we simply look at it without allowing the associative thought process to interfere.

The beauty of love is that you cannot do it, you cannot exercise it and you do not have to learn it. One of the outstanding characteristics of the qualities is that there is nothing to be learned, just as you do not need to learn to love. You cannot learn love; it is always present, and that is why whenever there is love, things are simple. Relationship is communication, and communication is consciousness in the form of thoughts, not description. If you think constantly about love and in the end you believe you are love, it is maya or illusion; it is not love. The motivative thought process breaks down consciousness into love, a color, the word *love* and then the movement of love. The illusion comes when you start the interpretation, the description of what you are communicating.

How does thinking that is based on the motivative thought process work?

Communication

The motivative thought process is simply communication. The motivative thought process is involved when you simply experience a particular situation, and when it is over, there is no associative thought process being activated into providing a description, thinking about how to interpret it, asking yourself why someone behaved as they did and so on.

If you are asked to think about a traumatic experience from your past, you may start to feel stressed, upset or even fearful. The brain cannot make the distinction between thinking of a situation and having something occur in the reality that is now. Whenever you think about the incident, the brain will react in exactly the same way as if it were to be again immersed in the traumatic experience. This will stimulate the production of adrenaline, which will in turn stimulate an increase in the hormone cortisol to counteract the effects of the adrenaline re-creating the same stress on the body experienced physiologically. This process will, over time, make the brain feel overloaded, and this will obstruct its ability to be alert and vital.

A study was done on forty adults who were classified as having had traumatic experiences in childhood, ranging from sexual abuse to torture. One child was chained to her bed by her parents for four years. The researchers could not find any trace of the trauma left within them, and they were interested in how these people had managed to heal so completely. Not only were they able to live full and happy lives, they showed unusual depth of character, wisdom and empathy. They showed none of the usual posttraumatic symptoms like hypervigilance, hyperarousal, insomnia, flashbacks or nightmares. They all said that they did not dwell on the past and had put their experience behind them. The usual psychological explanation for this would be that they had repressed their experiences, and the repression would show up again when confronted with a threat to their safety.

The second thing that the people in the study had in common was that they were totally absorbed in what they were doing. Traditional psychology would call this escaping into work. In psychospiritual terms, the diagnosis of escaping into work as a defense would be accurate only if a person had other trauma-related symptoms, reactions and compensatory behavior. They were simply living with the motivative thought process, i.e., direct communication with the world, and totally absorbed in what they were doing.

The third thing they all had in common was that they acknowledged that they were totally aware of what had happened to them. They were not focusing their energy on asking why it had happened to them; they simply had a direct relationship to it. There was no interpretation of it whatsoever, no questioning of the meaning of it, just an acknowledgement that it had happened.

These people also had similar temperaments and attitudes to life. As children they had problems at school because they were hyperactive, creative and wanted more stimulation. They constantly wanted to learn about things. They were not lazy. Laziness is not only about being physically inactive; it shows itself also in the way you create boredom for yourself with habits like never trying anything new. When asked about their experiences, they were ready to talk about what had happened but were not interested in blaming or analyzing. Asked whether she thought it had a meaning, and if she thought that she had learned anything from it, the woman who had been chained to her bed by her parents said simply that it had happened, and it is now over and that for her that was the end of it.

Another study was done on a hundred children from different European countries. According to psychological assessment they had had a difficult early life from birth until five years of age. They were reassessed at fourteen years old to assess their progress. Remember that between the ages of three and eight the qualities of a child are at their most active; therefore, this can be one of the strongest and most rebellious phases if the qualities are repressed. This happens again during puberty where rebelliousness in connection with repression of the qualities can occur.

It was found that in using their qualities they had built up a shield of resistance in order to protect themselves. So these children had their qualities intact and did not have a trace of hurt inside. The qualities acted as a form of protection from that hurt. They possessed three attitudes called the protection attitudes, which all served to protect their qualities.

The first attitude is commitment. If these fourteen-year-olds said something, you could rely totally on them to see it through – they had total commitment. The mystics always said that only when you are ready to go totally into something is there a movement away from the I. This movement away from the ego, from the associative thought structure, is the only protection you really have. Remember again the sayings of the mystics and all the religions about awareness being one of the best protective shields for the qualities. It does not matter whether the commitment is to God, to a person or to work just as long as you are totally in it without any "buts." Part of this has to do with having inner discipline.

The second attitude is control, in the old sense of the word. Control in the old sense of the word is not suppression; it is understanding and awareness at the same time. These children were absolutely clear about

what they wanted to say, how they said it, how they moved. This awareness is in all of us – it merely becomes atrophied as one gets older
because it gets overshadowed with all the "shoulds" and "musts" of
socialization.

The third attitude is that whenever they had to deal with things that
they were familiar with, they got bored quickly. They had the attitude
of being adventurous. In psychological terms it would be called the
ability to go forward and to deal with new things that they did not
understand or that they did not know about.

Acknowledging without description

For your own health and happiness, your brain has to realize how thinking works. You have to make a clear distinction between the thought
process that is communion with whatever is present and the thought
process that is pure description, i.e. between the motivative and the
associative process. At the same time, there needs to be a radical shift
in the way that we deal with thoughts. How can you learn to see thought
as a flower of consciousness if you are constantly moving in the associative thought process?

How will you ever get back to the qualities if you structure yourself
continuously in space and time? Remember that space-time is the past
and the future, or thought is fear. By acknowledging whatever has happened without moving into description we can maintain a direct communication with whatever is present. Looking for causes is pure
speculation because a cause is connected with time, and time is connected with the associative thought process and is therefore a breakdown of communication. The moment you begin to describe, you forget that thought grows out of consciousness, and you become lost in
thoughts. If we focus instead on the qualities, which are connected to
the medium of consciousness or the energy body, the outcome is completely different.

CHAPTER 6

The Movement of Energy

There are two levels of energy. There is the subtle body energy, which is the aura, and there is the energy body, which is the qualities or soul. The moment we start to focus our energy too much on the past, which in reality no longer exists, we create an energetic blockage or slow-down. All that precious energy that could be harnessed to simply observe our feelings and emotions without attaching a history to them gets absorbed in explanations and justifications and in recreating the same feeling patterns over and over again with no useful or helpful consequences.

To put it differently, subtle energy always follows thought. Remember that we need to distinguish between mind consciousness and out-of-body consciousness. This means that there is no energy movement without thought or intent providing the initiation of energy – we need the mind consciousness to get to the out-of-body consciousness that can exist without thought.

The subtle energy or *qi* or whatever you may wish to call it is always there; the fact that it follows thought means that thought is necessary for initiating the movement of energy. There is nothing wrong with thought, but we need to know how to use it properly. Subtle energy follows thought, and the energy body or qualities, if it is allowed to, always follows love. Love is not energy – it is the substance, the essence, of the out-of-body consciousness.

In terms of how energy moves, aggression is always a symptom of fear. Aggression never occurs without being preceded by a feeling of fear on the psychological level, which we need to remember is different from the biological kind of fear that we would naturally feel when, for example, a bomb is dropped in the street where we live. The latter produces a reflex on the biological level, which is a natural response to sudden shock. Whenever we avoid sadness we automatically create fear. Let us look at the relationship between sadness, fear and aggression.

All human beings (and possibly animals) have the structure of fear and then aggression. If we feel aggressive, which inevitably accompanies a feeling of fear, and if we relate the aggression to our personal history, we build up a fixation that just adds to the problem. In people who for some reason have become constantly fearful and almost never feel aggression, the fear or aggression then moves inward, as in cases of paranoia.

The second possible outcome of associating the aggression with a personal history is that we begin to blame ourselves or someone else. In blaming and creating guilt, we are still fundamentally feeling aggression – blame and guilt can be seen to be different channels or routes between fear and aggression. We can see how aggression is a symptom of fear, and guilt is simply a branch that stems out of aggression. The moment we start to feel aggressive and we limit it by relating it to our past, we are in fact only creating more aggression which can manifest in different ways.

A personal structure such as aggression or guilt can never be traced toward the future – it can only be traced toward the past, and so in interpreting aggression we are bound to go into the past. But the movement into the past is a movement in the I, which is bound by the constraints of space and time. Let us say you discover, and see it as an explanation, that your aggression comes from your father who did not love you – that is what your aggression seems to be about. This will lead you to always be very quick to defend yourself against your aggression. This act of having to defend something stems from the fear of not being understood.

With such an interpretation, where is our energy going? The "mental aura" is in a constant movement, and when we are experiencing aggression we are connected or moving with the personality/ego, which means we are bound to create an energetic connection to our past. If our attention is going into this kind of investigation into the past, the energy is going into something that no longer exists and it may even go into an illusionary picture of our past. This processes only tires and weakens our system further.

Energy and the mind

The mind is a brilliant instrument, and it consists of only 10 percent of the brain; the other 90 percent of the brain is used in dealing with the various physiological functions of the body. The most primitive, instinctual and earliest developed parts of the brain are specifically body oriented in contrast to the most recently evolved and sophisticated cortex.

The primitive reptilian brain is responsible for maintaining the most basic body systems, including reflexes, blood pressure and breathing. Within the relatively narrow parameters that support life, the reptilian brain includes the spinal cord, brain stem and cerebellum. The next level, called the paleomammalian brain, consists of the limbic system. Sometimes called the leopard brain, this system acts as a crude emotional-memory center that coordinates sensory input and reactions. The well-known fight-or-flight response comes from this part of the brain and includes the amygdala, hippocampus, thalamus and corpus callosum among other structures. It generates urges, appetites and emotions but not self-conscious awareness of these emotions. This self-reflective role lies in the neomammalian brain, the most recently evolved layer that includes the convoluted folds of the cerebral cortex and neocortex. These labyrinthine surfaces permit a huge increase in the number of interconnections among neurons, which yield what we usually think of as the higher mental functions: abstract thought, planning, complex memories, language and our ongoing, autobiographical sense of the self.

Emotions are always present on the body level and in the process of evolution; emotions played a very important part in human survival. Before joy there was fear, as without fear there can be no survival. Before love there was simply attention, the art of being aware. Love follows awareness, so it is structured in our being at the very beginning of existence, but it needs a vehicle to carry it within the material world, and this vehicle is the body-mind.

Understanding things intellectually is not necessary for survival. Even love is not necessary for survival. This whole area of emotions and feelings can be confusing – there is confusion between fast feelings and slow feelings; confusion between words and pictures; confusion between reason, sense and communication. Let us first look at slow feelings in their interaction with fast feelings and words in their interaction with pictures and symbols. Fast feelings are reactive, based on fear – for example, anger, rage, guilt, jealousy and other forms of aggression – and these fast feelings are felt on the body level and described commonly as emotions. What seems to be lacking is the connection to slow feelings.

Slow and fast feelings

Modern research shows that the cortex, or the thinking brain, has no part in fast feelings. Fast feelings are related to the amygdala part of the brain – the emotional center involved in survival – which can bypass or even "hijack" the cortex in heightened emotional situations. This means that we endlessly repeat fast feelings or emotions by nourishing them in thought structures one and two.

If our time here is for learning how to control our emotions, yet everything we do "triggers" our emotions, How do we get out of the fast cycle?

Slow feelings such as compassion, love, joy, inner peace and stillness are a process of expansion, growth and happiness – elements that are not necessary for survival and that are entirely structured in the neo-cortex and also over the heart energy center.

It would be dangerous to create a duality here by saying, for example, that aggression is bad and nonaggression is good, or that fear in general is bad and that we need to become less afraid. On the biological level, living without fear would be like having a body that cannot feel pain. Even on the psychospiritual level, fear, if we look at it positively, is the movement of creating awareness. Until now we have looked at fear negatively in associating it with the future, the unknown and the idea that it indicates danger and the presence of something that is against us. If we look at fear in terms of a quality or its positive aspect, it creates awareness and helps us move toward a state of being fully present. When we are able to observe the fast feelings related to fear, it naturally moves to the slow feelings of caring and love, and there can then be a sense of present awareness without fear. If we are honest with ourselves, most of us are awakened by fear and not by love.

Fast feelings and evolution

Evolution and modern society depend to some extent on the generation of fast feelings. We are still attached to such things as driving at high speed, dangerous activities like mountain climbing and sports like football, all of which trigger fast feelings. Whenever we identify with something, we automatically create fast feelings – for example, if we try to stay detached while watching a game of football by just enjoying watching the ball jump around the field, it would be quite boring, but if we identify with a team, it immediately becomes interesting and exciting.

We create and nurture fast feelings by thinking and identification – the associative thought process triggers the amygdala or emotional center in the brain. By observing how a human brain works in the course of one day, we learn that 70 percent of the time it is immersed in thought structure one, which has to do with the past and the future. More than half of this 70 percent tends to be pure fantasy, and only 1 percent relates to reality.

However, when you look at the world around you and see what human beings have created through the process of thought, you realize that art, theater, music and technology are the result of thought structures one and two. Inventions and works of art are created by a relatively small number of people. If we try to stop having fast feelings, the result is that our creativity is also suppressed; instead, we need to encourage our creativity by also getting in touch with our slow feelings.

Balance

If we look at religion, for example, over the last five thousand years, we see that there were very few key figures who had true wisdom. In the field of philosophy, there were very few in the last two thousand years who created something truly original. Plato and Socrates had one very important thing in common with Patanjali: they did not make a distinction between slow and fast feelings. Or to put it more simply, they were only interested in wanting to observe whatever came up.

Not even the pope has it

wisdom comes from?

anyone can do this.

The question is not whether fast feelings are good or bad – they are created by our biology, and not a single fast feeling can survive without being nourished by thoughts. If fast feelings were no longer to exist, it would mean that our whole hormonal system would fall apart. The question is, as Patanjali put it, "Can I move with them, without nourishing them?" Can I leave them on the body level without increasing them with thoughts?

The whole notion of measurement is borne out of thought structure two. Whenever thought structure two comes into play, even with the best of intentions you will be held back from moving on. It is not that fast feelings have to be controlled, but the slow feelings should also be allowed to manifest. So, for example, aggression in itself is not a bad thing, but love also needs to be present.

E ———→ Motion
slow it down Here

This does not mean that we are given carte blanche to do whatever we want to. It means that as long as your actions are based on measurement, or dominated by thought structure two, whatever you do – even if you do your best – will somehow be flawed. It is easy to make judgments such as "the world is bad," "people are bad," and therefore we need to save the world. To be motivated in this way is derived from thought structure two and is not helpful in the long run.

So fast feelings are not a weakness; they are only triggered or activated by our history. Thinking that they are weaknesses brings us to a cause-and-effect structure and to thinking that if we had not had this history then we would not be victim to these fast feelings. This is completely incorrect; fast feelings are part of the way the physical body is structured, part of our biology. The slow feelings are connected to the development of the third brain, the cortex, and are not connected with survival.

LOVE IS !

Slow feelings and reality

Every society has the duty to ensure that people have enough food, shelter and a basic quality of existence if we are to allow slow feelings to manifest in all of us. For example, giving young people the possibility of going to a university and to then use their talents when they leave becomes a basic necessity that can harness their potential to be loving, peaceful or to have awareness. Any society that does not value education is simply misguided. When you have to fight for your existence, it is difficult to feel joyful, caring, compassionate or to have inner peace.

When your very existence is in danger, which means that there is no perspective in your life, the body is bound to react, and so fast feelings will take over. It is not whether you have attained higher levels of consciousness that determines whether slow feelings become present. It is a question of whether you have any perspective in this life, and a large part of this perspective is determined by how society deals with providing for your basic needs.

The Hindus tried to solve the dilemma of inequality between people by creating the caste system in which people are encouraged to believe that they are born into misery because of misdeeds in their past lives. This forces people into postponing any possibility of self-fulfillment until the next life, denying them any possibility for transformation here and now. The body needs to live in the here and now, not in the next life. The quality aura is not influenced by fast feelings, so it is of no help to wait for the next life. The mind, in an attempt to solve this problem, invented the associative thought process. The associative thought process creates meaning where there is, in reality, no meaning. It is a beautiful tool for survival, but it is also based on illusion. If we look at the power of the Egyptians, the Greeks or the Romans, for example, we see how this sort of power is only temporary because a lot of energy is always absorbed in trying to hold on to power.

Real power – the power of the spiritual master, the shaman, the white magician or the mystic – is simply the ability to create your own reality. The rest is bound to fall apart. The ability to create your own reality does not require an ability to look into the future. It simply requires us to know how to use the power of thought, and to do this our brain needs to work for us instead of against us. We need to differentiate between brain consciousness, or thinking, and out-of-body consciousness, which is independent of the brain and is characterized by a shift in perception away from the personal structure.

Heart and out-of-body consciousness

The physical aura is a vibration of body cells that creates an electrical-chemical movement, a form of light that can be seen around you; then there is the mental aura, the movement of brain cells, which creates brain waves; and finally the quality aura or out-of-body consciousness, which is not dependent on how the body works and doesn't change over time. It is connected to the soul consciousness and carries within it the potential of qualities that are available to us throughout our lives.

Out-of-body consciousness is anchored over the heart. It includes the heart as an organ and also the energy field surrounding the heart, or what is known as the heart chakra. The heart energetic field is almost two hundred times stronger than that of the brain. If all psychological problems are rooted in our relationship with ourselves, the balance between the energy body or the quality aura and the subtle body or mind consciousness happens over the heart. The balance comes about when we can see our feelings, such as aggression, fear and guilt, as a process independent of our history. From this less personalized position, we can more easily access this heart energy, and as higher energy penetrates deeper levels there follows a huge shift of perception. When we can look at something without a description there is stillness, and out of this stillness energy is created, bringing vitality with it. This whole process needs to be experienced rather than understood.

When I can look at Tim without catching History, pain, I be still in my heart..

The process of understanding why, for example, someone behaves a certain way, or the process of understanding a language, requires an investment of time and energy. Understanding does not work on the psychospiritual level because understanding is always a movement of logic and on the psychospiritual level, there is no logic. Understanding involves a hierarchical movement, whereas on the spiritual level there is absolutely no authority or hierarchy and therefore no logic.

Similarly, love cannot be understood. If we experience a change in our perspective that makes it possible for us to begin to see and acknowledge how love, as an atmosphere of the qualities, is already present at the beginning of life, this cannot be understood logically. You can study love for as long as you want, but it simply cannot be understood. You have read things about love, you have heard things about love, you have reflected about love, but this does not increase your capacity to love; it does not make it any stronger. You may be able to understand a feeling, specifically the fast feelings, and even this is a difficult thing to do. Slow feelings do not involve any process of understanding. We are extremely entrenched in the notion that nothing can be achieved without first gaining some understanding of things.

I have "experienced" this NOT to be true.

Joy cannot be understood, and bliss is simply a movement, an accident that does not arise because of you – it is not personal and has nothing to do with your past experience. Love and joy are not structured in time. The same goes for nirvana, enlightenment or whatever you may wish to call it – these concepts all represent the same thing and that is love. Remember that love, joy and bliss all belong to the group of slow feelings.

Energy and thought structure three
If energy follows thought, then brain or mind consciousness and out-of-body consciousness are both interactive and separate. We can see how brain consciousness or thinking may create our problems, but it cannot solve them. If we don't connect with the out-of-body consciousness or qualities, this leads to rebellious qualities or weaknesses being predominant. These rebellious qualities are simply the qualities trying to flow through us. It follows that weaknesses are in fact part of the qualities, and they can be integrated into the qualities by connecting with the timeless observer – with the movement toward thought structure three.

Getting in touch with thought structure three can be done only when we are in a state of stillness. Psychologically, stillness implies the absence of fear. Spiritually and in psychospiritual terms it is about focusing not on the content of our thoughts but on how thought functions. In this way we are able to make a distinction between the different levels of thinking, and in the process space is created in the brain. Stillness does not necessarily mean that you must sit and meditate.

Very often, meditation creates more unrest than stillness. Stillness is a function of your relationship to your brain and your mind. As we saw earlier, when we are preoccupied with form, time and the ego, we are within thought structures one and two. This kind of thinking gives rise to the idea that because I am of form, i.e., my body is a form, so my ego must be form too – I am history; therefore, what happens next must also be a question of cause and effect.

What really happens next is the automatic limitation of yourself to the most basic level of your manifestation. This is due partly because the quality aura is difficult to sense and feel. We therefore limit ourselves to only what we can see and feel, just like the doubter in the Christian tradition, the Apostle who does not believe in Christ. If we believe only in what we are able to see, we will never see the whole. However, if we start believing in things we cannot see, this too can create problems.

When we are listening to a piece of music that we like, for example, the feeling of liking the music is not something we can see, and it is very often not something we can fully express either. Or something that often happens in relationships is that women ask men to tell them what they feel about the relationship and to describe it in words. Men usually say, "I do not know." Our need to understand in a rational way is actually a barrier to developing relationships, as it is a process of wanting to structure whatever is present according to our history, to form and to time.

If we take the usual approach, we try to understand what is going on. There is a paradox here: if it is true that there is nothing to understand, then why read this book? On the other hand, if we never reflect, then we will not understand and we will not reach a state of being. The trick is to never take for granted whatever we hear or reflect on as the truth; instead, see it as a movement of information. Remember the Zen master telling his students, "If I point to the moon with my finger, do not look at the finger." To really understand also means that we need to be able to make choices, and to do this we need to make definitions and comparisons. Understanding is always part of thought structure two. Try for a moment to listen without trying to understand.

In Time Therapy, we call this the art of *direct observation* or *direct seeing*. To see an aura, for example, is a direct process where absolutely no knowledge and no measurement is required. Try to read this sentence without attempting to fully understand its meaning: energy follows thought, and thought follows love. It is a process of direct seeing, with no obscurations or interference of thought.

Direct observation

If we can consciously use our mind to observe our own behavior, in the process of conscious presence and observation of our mind, body, thoughts and feelings, we can sense that there is something more spacious behind this, which we call the timeless observer. We can change to the timeless observer state simply by moving the mind-observer away from the field of body/thought/feeling toward a state of "conscious absence," a state in which one moves between "being" with awareness and "not being." In this state, our eyes are open and we observe what is happening in ourself without allowing a description of what is seen to become dominant.

This observer is clearly different from thought structures one and two and only partially belongs to the fore-future. We cannot grasp or define the timeless observer. We can only learn to observe it infinitely – whenever we try to grasp the timeless observer, we find it is limitless, endless and indefinable. It is what we really are, and it belongs to psychospiritual consciousness.

The atmosphere of the observer

If thought cannot control thought, and thought is always the process of description, then something that has been created by thought cannot be solved by thought. Most things are created by thought – the idea of who you are, what you should be, why you are the way you are. If what you think you are is the creation of thought, and you try to understand or solve this through thought, you will then simply create more tension and more pressure. The mind must see that there is another way. If it is in the nature of the mind not to be able to deal with things that are beyond space and time, then obviously it can never hope to find a real answer to the problems that are its own creation, namely thoughts. It can never really be in touch with consciousness. It can only be in touch with the manifestations of consciousness.

Our constant challenge is: How can we access our fullest potential to be able to perceive wider dimensions of consciousness, and, more importantly, how can this help us to improve the quality of our daily life? If energy follows thought, and thought follows love, how can we use the energy that is always available to us to see that we can experience our true consciousness? And what is in the way of putting this into practice?

A problem can only be solved when the quality is able to manifest. Uncovering the cause of your problems may make you feel better because the problem is no longer focused on you, but this insight will not guarantee that your qualities will become manifest. The mind knows without understanding or being able to grasp it that thought originates from consciousness. How can it get to this state of realization so that fear, which is represented by the future and which thought always wants to control, can take another perspective without using the vehicle of thought? The mind realizes that it cannot make one movement or have one thought without there being something that is aware of the thought or the movement. It realizes that there is an observational part that is constantly present that observes everything one does, thinks or feels.

This observer could also be called the witness. The moment you try to observe the observer, it slips away from you. The moment you try to observe the observer, there is the observer observing the observer. It is impossible to try to give a name to this observer who is observing. It is endless; you cannot control it. This is what it means to be out of space-time. It is like the traditional concept of God as someone who is watching over his children all the time, but there is no one really watching you – the witness is interconnected with your own mind; it is not a totally separate entity. As the Buddha said, we are all interconnected, and everything we do, everything we are, arises in relationship to something or someone.

are-os is not discipline

is this like an outlook or only of body?

So what might happen if the mind, instead of trying to control a thought with thoughts, just switches to the observer? If the mind suddenly gets in touch with that which is unnameable, which is always endless and which is not structured according to personality, the future suddenly disappears.

The whole structure of fear disappears, and when there is no fear, there is no need for control. The incredible thing is that we all know this happens, that whatever we do, feel or think, there is something somewhere observing all of it. This process happens naturally to us all when we go to sleep, for example. *Except may be for those who Continue to struggle "letting go" even while sleeping, ie, jaw grinding, nightmares, endless tossing returning.*

The atmosphere of this observer is called love. We can stop controlling thoughts – not by trying to stop thoughts with thoughts but by shifting to the timeless observer. In doing this, the time barrier breaks down. The personality, the history or the identification falls away, and whenever this happens, love is present. In this movement there is no future to concern you. There is just the fore-future.

This is the most efficient "control" you can have over life, but it is not something that you can learn; you cannot exercise love, and it is not a feeling. Love is a state of being. It is always present when thought is not trying to control anything. The moment you want to control yourself, become better or be different, then you are no longer able to fall in love with yourself. Do not fall in the trap of feeling that you have to accept yourself. Who is going to do the accepting? It is thought that is trying to convince you to accept yourself, and this is a process involving control. Do not fall in the trap of the so-called esoteric way that urges you to "let go." Who is going to let go? It is thought trying to let go, and this is also a process involving control.

Thought originates out of consciousness and cannot control itself. Trying to control thought leads to a fruitless struggle to define what is good or bad and to get rid of unwanted elements in yourself. Instead, shift your awareness to the observer, and you will experience the relationship between the observer that is observing your body, mind, aura, feeling, thoughts and environment. You will then get in touch with the observer that is observing the observer and the endless chain of witnessing and with the process of depersonalization.

Once you see that thought cannot control thought and switch to the observer, then you will see that all your weaknesses, the so-called problems, are in fact not produced by the past but are part and parcel of being human. The fear of the future, of not having control over the future, is present in every human being in differing situations and contexts. The structure of your problem is the nature of fear and is something that is not personal to you alone. In seeing this you create a relationship to it, and after this you will find yourself switching to the reference of the observer.

If you are able to see the problem and the history of this problem but without switching to the observer, you then end up simply dealing with the illusion that your thoughts will solve the problem. Through depersonalization the problem dissolves and looks completely different because the mind can see that whatever happens to it, it has not only an individual aspect, just as the body does, but an aspect beyond this individuality that is much more significant. The habitual mind believes that because it has developed such incredible structures of thought, it can also solve the problems of the I/ego through thought. From the standpoint of the mind, quality of life depends on getting rid of all the weaknesses, not realizing that in doing this you would simply end up dead. Perfection is a myth; it is not a reality. For the mind to stop fighting against weaknesses involves changing the focus from the weaknesses to a focus on the observer. The weaknesses then become part of the qualities. Fear becomes a signal to be attentive to what is happening to you, while sadness becomes this tremendous energy that transforms into love. ? *Don't get connection here.*

If you try to get rid of fear, then you just cannot feel love because fear is the symptom of sadness, and sadness is a tremendous energy that brings you directly to compassion. If you want to get rid of sadness and try to do this through personalizing it, or through looking for a past explanation for your sadness, you simply create self-pity.

Awareness, inner peace and energy

Psychological fears and problems can be dealt with best by cultivating awareness and inner peace, which are mutually dependent on each other. Awareness is the absence of judgment, comparison and interpretation. Awareness is the timeless observer, observing without reaction. Inner peace is the knowledge or understanding that in the end, everything has a "depersonalized" character and is independent of all identification. Inner peace leads to a state of not reacting.

Together, they are the strongest instruments for developing a wider and clearer consciousness detached from the ego. If you see them as a definition, however, and not as a process, or do not understand the deeper meaning to them, they become useless tools. Awareness cannot be used to get out of a state of fear because the more fear there is, the less awareness there can be. Simply observe that awareness is the possibility of thinking without words. Most of the thinking you do is in language and therefore is connected with the learning and use of a language. Awareness is the ability to think without the use of words and language, which means that it does not then allow you to give the fear that is present a definition or a description.

Psychological fear is a fast feeling, which means that there is an input of adrenaline into the body. It lasts for one minute at the most and then disappears, so to keep this fear alive you then need to activate it through thinking. You have to nourish and encourage the fear with your thoughts. Every feeling and emotion is related to the mental structure, which is directly connected with the quality aura. We need the mental structure to recognize the quality aura, so the body becomes a channel: the body cannot be separated from the mind, and body-mind cannot be separated from space and time. Once you can see that the quality aura has nothing to do with and is not influenced by what is happening in the body-mind structure, you will reach a turning point in how you deal with your body-mind. You will suddenly fall out of the implications of time.

For example, say you call your husband's office at around 8:00 in the evening because he told you that he would be working late. A colleague who has no idea what your husband told you answers the phone and tells you that he left at 4:00, saying that he was going home. Laughingly, the colleague remarks that he may of course have popped out with the secretary whom he seems fond of. On hearing this your adrenaline immediately rushes in, whoosh, but after one minute the adrenaline is no longer physiologically present in the body, and so you have to bring in thoughts and fantasy in order to fuel the process of being upset. You have to nourish the fear, and because the brain is a fantastic instrument, you can artificially activate a little more adrenaline within your system with coffee, a little sugar or cigarettes.

There are many different ways of activating worry artificially, but all of this takes place within your mind, and all of it can be transformed through simple awareness. If you can cultivate being aware without using words, you will find yourself in a total relationship with your whole being. When there is no description, slow feelings can emerge, and once a relationship is established to whatever is there, there is always a shift in energy. As the awareness gets stronger and there is a growing sense of absence of time, the more you will be in a direct relationship and flow with whatever is happening.

Culture of feelings
is embracing ALL feelings

Hate
Anger
isolation
Drepression   *embrace*
                  understand
                  release
                  Balance

CHAPTER 7

Awareness and the Qualities

So far we have seen that personal history is not as important as it seems, that we need to change how we think rather than what we think and to learn how to direct our awareness toward our true consciousness, our strengths or qualities. We realize that all our weaknesses are shared by everybody else; they are just more evident in some people than in others because of particular events in their past. So it makes sense for us to work with our strengths rather than our weaknesses. Our qualities have a direct connection with the observing faculty of our mind; as far as our thinking is concerned, they are by far the clearest structure we have, and the qualities alone can create a perspective on life.

Shifting the focus

The more the qualities are present, the more they absorb our weaknesses, just as the dark is absorbed into the light when we flick a switch. Imagine you are standing in a dark room holding a flashlight, directing the light onto your heart area. A tiny beam of light is going into your body, but the darkness around you remains. If you were to turn the flashlight around and move it away from you, the darkness would simply disappear. Now that there is light, you feel pleased to be able to see and can get on with whatever it is you need to do. If you were to return the flashlight to its original position, focused entirely on your body, the darkness would return. It is really as simple as that.

If you blame someone for something that happened in your life, eventually you have to imagine what it was like to be the person you are blaming, to look at what happened to that person. If your mother was abused by her father, we have to ask what was happening in his life and in his parents' lives; we might have to go back generations. If you see yourself just from your individual perspective, you remain within the prison, and the chain never gets broken. As Jesus said, let he who has done no wrong cast the first stone. Someone has to break the chain.

When the Buddha referred to karma, he meant that freedom comes only through breaking the illusion of a chain of action and reaction. Do not look back at your life for explanations because you will find an endless chain of cause and effect. It is far better to create a perspective. Creating a perspective is the act of cutting the chain of illusion. Your individual history does not hold the whole truth; from the perspective of depersonalization, we all go through the same thinking processes, but because we depend on our past for a sense of who we are, we very often fail to recognize this simple truth.

Balance of feelings

As energy follows thought, higher energy always penetrates lower energy but never the other way around. We are always much more than our weaknesses. In the case of serious illness, for example, for as long as you continue to live, although it may be unpleasant, only the weaker part – the body – is affected. If you are in physical or psychological pain, and if you try to just observe it without feeding it with thoughts and feelings about it and what the implications might be, the witnessing part of your mind becomes independent of the pain. The best way to keep your immune system in balance is not only through diet, healthy living and relaxation. If every morning you wake up and feel grateful for your health, it is like praising someone who is doing a job well. If it could, the immune system would react positively to this. When we begin to look for solutions, it is more helpful to connect with our strengths or qualities rather than try to work out why we are as we are.

Asking the right questions

The past is always subjective. Your memory is never representative of the total reality of what happened. Again, if the thinking processes are shared by everybody, then while the past influences your mind, it is not responsible for how you think. If we focus on the process of thinking, on that which we truly are and on the observer, the past suddenly loses its power. We become aware that our problems now are not solely a result of our own individual history and isolation and that how we are in the world now has come about largely through misunderstanding ourselves.

This is sooo me!

It is important that we avoid working with the process of *why*. Why am I like this? Why are things as they are? Always work with the process of "How is it?," "What is the movement of it?" Not "Why am I jealous?" but "What is jealousy?" The processes involving *why* always lead back into the past, while the inquiry into *how?* and *what?* always lead to a perspective, to an expansion, to an opening rather than a closing down, to new beginnings rather than to endings or conclusions. So do not even ask "Why should I ask these questions?" because at least 50 percent of your energy will be absorbed in observing whether or not you have gained anything by asking "How is it?" It will create a duality, which will split your energy in two.

Problems are truly solved by listening and creating a relationship to the qualities, or the energy body. Listening and observing creates the movement of relationship. In order to understand ourselves or anyone else we need to listen and observe. As we have said already, all problems are in the end shared by each and every one of us; they only have different contents and descriptions. Understanding yourself comes not by working on yourself or by analyzing because the one who analyzes is the same as the one who has the problem and therefore cannot really see what is happening. It is the connection to the quality aura through

listening and observing that creates understanding. Gradually it becomes clear that the future is created by the past because the degree to
which you are in touch with your qualities now will affect how your
past unfolds. Solutions do not come through analyzing cause and effect; they come through using your qualities. Treat yourself with care
as you would a two-year-old child. You would not ask why it is doing
whatever it is doing; you would just try to understand what is happening and act according to whether or not it needs to be protected or if
you can give it space to be.

Listening is part of stillness. Listen to yourself. If you sense that you
are listening to an outside source, this is because the outside is just a
vibration that is activating part of the whole system. Whenever there
is a meeting of different levels of energy bodies, or different qualities,
each vibration will add to whatever is present to give rise to something
more than itself. Listening on this level is like putting together a jig-
saw puzzle. No one person knows the whole truth and can express it;
there are millions of people who when they are in touch with their
qualities or quality auras, their consciousness or the soul aspect, or
whatever you may wish to call it, will add to the puzzle so as to produce a oneness.

What are the qualities?

When we think, our thoughts originate in consciousness, and consciousness is the quality aspect of our being. Happiness is a state of
being when the qualities are manifested through the body-mind. Instead of continuously being focused on our weaknesses, on trying to
understand the negative, how can we start to reorient toward our qualities, which will then translate into increasing awareness?

Typically, and specifically from its point of view of being structured
for survival, the mind says: if with the help of thought I can control
what happens in the body (for example, fighting off illness by a mind-
over-matter approach or positive thinking), then I must also be able to
control psychological things through thinking. This is like thought

trying to control thought. The tragedy is that, in fact, thought cannot control thought, and trying to do this will only cause more psychological and physical problems. The immune system, for example, gets weakened when thought tries to control thought, and in an extreme case there might be depression, psychotic states, nervous breakdown or classical paranoia. All obsessions are simply extremes of thought trying to control thought. Fortunately, most of us are not moved to the point where we display such symptoms, but we can still feel depressed or unhappy, or just feel that something is not right, and to start an inquiry into what is really happening, we need to get in touch with our consciousness, or soul energy.

Soul consciousness

The first thing that comes into existence when one is born is an energy that is the atmosphere of the soul, our true consciousness, Buddha-nature or the quality aura; we come into the world full of our true essential nature of innocence, beauty and love. The quality aura has to immediately interact with four other levels, and that is what the process of birth means. The four levels are the body, the parents, society and actual situations.

The energy of the quality aura must adapt to the material world, or gravity, which appears like a black hole as far as our true essence is concerned. However, in spite of all this gravity, the essence cannot be destroyed. It is constantly knocking at the door of our being, and the real miracle is that whatever we may do we cannot escape our qualities, our potential. When we contact the quality aura through simple awareness, it permeates the whole aura structure, including our mental and emotional bodies. The quality aura is that last part of us to dissolve after death.

Why do qualities get lost?

Weaknesses develop because we have a heightened attachment to our body-mind, despite the fact that the qualities are our true nature. By not being in touch with our qualities, we increase our awareness of the obstacles, or blockages, to our potential. This is then followed by an interpretation of these blockages, of why we cannot do something, for example, and because this interpretation is produced by the brain consciousness, it is to a large extent mistaken. We need to listen with our inner intelligence, with part of the energy body rather than a function of the brain.

By now you might be saying: hang on a second, if from the very beginning the qualities are knocking on the door of one's being and if they can never be totally repressed, what about the evil deeds that people do; what about Hitler, for example? When Hitler was young, he called himself the wolf, Adolph wolf. Later in life his greatest love was for wolves. By the age of ten, he was already saying that he had no choice other than to become a great leader. Of course, when a child tells you this you tend to think it is all fantasy, and as children most of us have fantasies of being successful. Nowadays, all the role models around us increase this urge. When Göring told Hitler to stop because the Russians would soon be in Berlin, Hitler replied, "I cannot choose to stop, even if I burn myself I cannot stop."

Having qualities is no guarantee of behaving ethically or morally. This is why all religions hand down ethical codes like the Ten Commandments of Jesus or the Buddha's Noble Eightfold Path. The difference between a black magician and a white magician is not that the white magician is better or has qualities that are more advanced; it is simply that his motivation is different. The direction that this motivation takes comes down to a question of ethics.

The qualities and gravity

If we can see this with empathy, which is the art of dealing with the energy behind our actions, then we realize why all the true spiritual teachers (especially the Christian mystics) emphasized the importance of forgiveness. We are encouraged to forgive even our worst enemy because there is no good and bad, or no duality. This is impossible for the mind to see; the mind is dependent on the brain, and the brain is nothing more than a huge instrument of measurement, where everything is divided into good or bad. The mind is unable to look at anything "bad" without judging it. Having or feeling empathy means you are able to acknowledge what it is like to be in the shoes of someone like Hitler without giving in and acting in the same way.

This is what each individual's quality aura has to do at birth: it has to live two lives at the same time. When you take away the measurement of good and bad, you suddenly realize that the description of good and bad is just a way for the mind to explain and understand quality and gravity. The essence manifesting in the material is what happens in every child at the moment of birth, and this immediately manifests as two lives, i.e., as the quality and the mind form. It has to adjust to gravity without losing sight of the qualities: an absolutely brilliant task. And when we say this quality never goes away, it means that it also never leaves the presence of someone like Hitler. All we can say is that he used his quality in a way that was structured too much in gravity.

We can see another example in love and sexuality. Love is independent from gravity; it is the medium or the instrument for the qualities to manifest and always involves moving away from ourselves toward another. On the level of gravity it shows as a mixture of love, a movement away but also a strong movement toward ourselves, because physical attraction is also involved, and we want our sexual needs to be met. However, if we integrate love too much into gravity, we have pure sexuality. The mystics simply used sexuality instead of God and the devil, instead of good and bad, as another way of trying to understand how one's essence can be structured too much on material levels. Not that there is anything wrong with pure sexuality, but it is simply a dead end.

The mystics constantly used symbols to show us this miracle, which is also our universal human predicament, and which is reflected in the ancient spiritual dilemma of how to be in the world but not of it. All this means is that we need to become aware of the psychospiritual pos-

sibilities in our lives. The Zen masters called it creating a balance between the essence – the qualities and all that is present at the beginning of life – and the structuring of it all in the body, the relationship
to parents, the environment and life situations.

If we do not develop an awareness of something beyond gravity, then
we may over time miss the whole point of our existence. This is what
Socrates meant by "Know thyself," the reasons behind the teachings
of Christ, the Buddha and all the spiritual traditions. The qualities can
easily be misused without the guiding force of an ethical structure. It is
better to misuse the qualities, however, even if we are motivated by the
material world, than not to use them at all. In psychological terms, it is
better to make mistakes than to keep yourself imprisoned in safety and
security because at least in the process of making the mistakes, you
have the possibility of waking up. *Boy Howdy !*

A child who is not allowed to make mistakes and who is required to be
perfect is like a flower that is not given the conditions in which to
bloom. A person who is not allowed to do wrong is a person who has
no space. It is simply impossible to grow and do everything correctly.
By making mistakes we develop our ethical standards. We can learn
from the example of the Buddha, who chose not to keep himself in the
richness and beauty of his father's palace but to go out into the world,
not because he had compassion but simply because he was curious. He
left the palace and saw how much suffering there was, which prompted
feelings of compassion together with an awareness of how we can free
ourselves from our self-created prisons.

Immediately when we are born we are confronted with the first conflict, but we are not really aware of it with our thoughts. Before thought
there is consciousness. If we ask what came first, thinking or language,
we find that language is followed by thinking. *? really ?*

only or
You think as a product of having learned a language. So first there is
consciousness, and it is never separated from awareness. To know, or

not the same as thinking)

to be in touch with yourself, is not the essence of awareness; it is simply a by-product of awareness.

Awareness is the essence of consciousness. For example, a baby is totally aware of itself – it does not think, "I realize this and that about myself, I know myself." What is this awareness if there is no thought? We constantly connect awareness and consciousness with our thoughts. Who or what is being aware in order that we can make this connection? We think and at the same time we are aware that we are thinking, and this is possible because we all have the energy body that has the capacity to be aware.

So the fundamental question at the moment of birth is not, "How do I treat this baby?" but "What mistakes am I making in my actions toward the baby; how much do I and the relationship I am in with my partner influence the baby? What can I do to ensure that the qualities do not fade away or become repressed?" In this way it becomes clear how we are not our problems. Throughout our lives we may have experienced difficulties that we put down to factors like poor education or lack of care from our parents, but essentially we are as we are simply because our qualities are repressed. The problems or the weaknesses are simply the other side of our obscured strengths – a symptom arising from the repressed qualities.

In a sense Hitler was desperately trying to bring his qualities to the surface. This sounds very difficult for us to accept, but the truth is that there is no problem nor weakness that does not represent a quality. Weaknesses occur naturally when a quality cannot be expressed. The energy body will always react when there is repression, which begins with the process of manifesting in the physical world. The parents are the first relationship, but the first form of repression is gravity, which is like putting on bad-fitting shoes. It will hurt a little and will be unpleasant.

In the Buddhist teachings, a bodhisattva is an enlightened being who is willing to stay on the planet, to remain in gravity, to help others until everyone is free, or living through their Buddha nature, which essentially means living their qualities. But we also have to help ourselves, and it is important not to accept the more fatalistic teachings of Hinduism, for example, which, to justify the caste system, say that we have chosen to be incarnated into this particular life, however miserable, because we have to learn something, or it is our karma.

In contrast and in opposition to the religious orthodoxy of his time, the Buddha taught the importance of self-inquiry and recommended a path of action, not acceptance, faith or belief. And much later, Karl Marx was one of the first who asked how the qualities could manifest while people lived in poverty. Marx turned on its head the concept of accepting one's fate whatever happens without fighting it. He said in an industrial society we simply cannot allow that to be. How can people listen, observe, create a relationship with their true nature if they have to fight for survival? How can a society be spiritual if we are focused on the fear of the future? When we become parents we do exactly what Marx said was necessary for the qualities to develop – we try to create an environment where our child does not have to fight for survival.

Manifesting the qualities

In common with the impact of the industrial era in the nineteenth century, the modern information age has created more mental stress and more competition in our lives. It may be that to know how to read and write is necessary for us all, but the system has gone far beyond this. Overloading the mental structure in a competitive way so that young people feel that their future depends solely on academic success results in the qualities being repressed. Having more information does not make us any happier; it just creates the illusion of a well-developed ego.

The strongest characteristic of our qualities is that they do not have to be learned; they are simply there. There is nothing you can do for them or against them. There is nothing you can add; there is nothing to exercise. If you want to know whether you are connected with a quality or with something else, it is very simple. The quality has no learning process; it has no time or space associated with achievement. There is absolutely no learning involved. Very simply, they can either be repressed or expressed. If the qualities are a state of being, it follows that whenever they cannot be manifest, there must be a reaction, a rebellion. When someone is physically imprisoned, it only creates anger and aggression. If people are not allowed to have choices, it creates frustration, and politically it will show as political unrest.

On the level of the mind, if the essence or being cannot be expressed, then it will somehow create other ways of manifestation, for example, in symptoms related to physical ailments or illnesses or psychological problems. If we use an artificial dam to keep water contained, one day the water will overflow because it wants to go its own way. Nature is a beautiful example of how we cannot destroy being; we can only create barriers around it. Higher energy always penetrates lower energy and not the other way around, which simply means that whatever we do, whatever we resist, higher energy will always triumph. We can repress our essential nature until the last moment of dying, but then it will become free. Whatever difficulties we are experiencing are nothing other than symptoms of our qualities trying to be released.

This is what is meant by enlightenment: simply that we give our being, or the qualities, all the credit for who we are. We let ourselves be guided by our true nature; we set ourselves free.

CHAPTER 8

Keys to Inner Freedom

Inner freedom refers to the part of us that is responsible only to our-selves. In reality there is no inner or outer freedom – inner freedom simply describes the kind of freedom that is not connected with the outside world politically or socially. In the outside world there is never complete freedom to do whatever we want. We spend a lot of time worrying about things connected with the outside world, and it is dif-ficult to feel free in the sense of being peaceful and happy. When we do experience a certain amount of peace and stillness, which means that nothing specific seems to be happening, the mind doesn't imme-diately relax and say, "This is exactly what I am looking for." What really happens when we experience this kind of stillness and freedom?

Obstacles to inner freedom
The first thing that happens is that we feel uneasy, followed by a feel-ing of boredom, and then, if we are perfectly honest, we have a sense of fear. Why, if we are constantly searching for that inner freedom, stillness, peace and happiness, do we become fearful when we find it? When we talk about a state of being in which there is freedom, we have to understand this from a biological point of view. We have to look at the huge problem of addiction that we all face – not just addic-

tion to alcohol or drugs but the real addiction of adrenaline that affects every one of us.

Remembering that body and mind cannot be separated, we see how the mind constantly needs action to give us an illusionary feeling of being awake. We are more compassionate and caring toward people who seem to be suffering than those who feel happy and joyful. Film, television programs and sports all boost our adrenaline levels.

Imagine for a moment that you are lying in bed feeling very relaxed despite everything that may be going on in your life. The best way to increase your adrenaline is to begin to worry about something that affects you or someone else. Many of the problems we worry about are not real problems at all but a way of providing us with an adrenaline input.

When our adrenaline levels go up we feel awake, aware and lively, but this feeling of being awake is not the awareness that the Buddha referred to. Instead, it is artificial and addictive. As soon as we feel good we fall asleep symbolically; when the shoes fit perfectly we no longer feel our feet. We are only aware of our body when something is wrong.

In 1991 during the Gulf War when the Iraqis were shooting missiles at Israel, two days before the first attack and for three days afterward, it was found that the number of deaths from natural causes had risen by 45 percent. But over the following week, the death rate went back to normal. The people who died were not even living near the danger zone. They were living in Tel Aviv or Jerusalem, and it was very unlikely that one of the missiles would land anywhere near them. This shows how the brain and its powers of visualization can create so much stress that the body may be irreparably harmed. It shows that the brain has an ability to focus on and influence the possibility of death without our being conscious of what is happening.

If our adrenaline levels are either too high or too low, we have a problem. There are countless other examples of how the mind has an influence on when we die, on how we deal with fear and worries and on how we deal with the addiction to adrenaline. When we ask why it is so difficult to reach inner freedom, we see how the mind is addicted to adrenaline, which means we are psychologically addicted to fear. Everybody says that they want to be rid of fear, but when there is no fear we feel unsettled. When there are absolutely no more worries, we are simply resting in stillness, but the mind will protest that something is wrong.

The mind and survival

The mind creates its own illusion in claiming that it wants to be free, which means peace, stillness and happiness, but when it comes close to the actual moment of surrender and peace, it immediately tries to escape from it. We are constantly cheating ourselves in this way – for example, we are afraid of getting into an enjoyable relationship and prefer to deal with the question of why we are not in a relationship, what might be wrong and so on.

If you can see how you are addicted to adrenaline, you will suddenly understand your problems from a different perspective. You will realize that if you dare to ignore your weaknesses you are in trouble, not because the weaknesses are a problem but simply because you will be in cold turkey with no more adrenaline pumping into your system.
The mind, the I, the ego is not there to relax; it is there to survive. Surviving is a question of either fight, flight or paralysis. Living in survival mode means first having a junglelike awareness where the mind is always hypervigilant and focusing on what might go wrong. How can a body, which is in connection with the mind and is constantly on the watch for what might go wrong, be able to relax? And how can a body, poisoned by the addiction to adrenaline if it ever did become relaxed, become free of the addiction?

If we really want to be in a state of inner peace and freedom, we have to get out of this addiction. There is now more information around than ever before on, for example, how we can learn to meditate, deal with our aggression, begin to understand others, improve our relationships and learn to love unconditionally. Has all this knowledge helped when we can see how in the case of real addiction to smoking, alcohol or heroin the will is always weaker than the addiction? The same is true for adrenaline. Using your will, you can try as hard as you like to be a nice person, to be loving or more forgiving – it will not really help, and all the spiritual advice about how one should be becomes simply a moral habit if the underlying addiction is not dealt with first.

How strong is your addiction to adrenaline? How quickly do you get frightened when there is stillness or peace or nothingness, as the mystics call it? How quickly do you get excited when something is happening? Take football, for example. People get excited when their team scores a goal, but if they were to constantly score goals, the supporters would get bored. The real excitement comes from the fear that they might lose. This is what creates the adrenaline buzz.

Addiction and fear

On the level of biological consciousness, we have a natural fear that is related to survival. To survive we need an input of energy, and this is created by adrenaline. The survival instinct is essential for life. Another fear on the level of psychobiological consciousness relates to not having enough food or where one is going to live. On the psycho-spiritual level there are three fears that are connected with habit and addiction. We are afraid of other people and whether or not they love us and accept us. Most of us have great ideas, most of us receive information that we could put into action, but the fear of not being accepted by others blocks our potential and our expression.

We are afraid of our own thoughts and feelings. We feel we may not know enough, or maybe we are mistaken or insecure about the beliefs we hold. We are so afraid of our feelings that even when it comes to feelings of love, we tend to hold them back. And we are afraid of death and dying. We deal with all of this by keeping busy, for which we need adrenaline. Being busy provides us with a distraction, which stops us from being really aware of these fears on the psychospiritual level. This is a brilliant strategy for the mind but a disaster when it comes to the question of finding inner peace, freedom, stillness, love and compassion.

Fear of death   *The Unknown*

Most of us tend to put off facing up to the fact that we will die someday. We are all masters in the art of avoidance. We don't know when, how or where it will happen; and it is one of our greatest fears in life. Even religious tradition encourages us to believe that death exists only in the future – if we feel unhappy in this life and believe in reincarnation, we can always hope for an easier life next time or hold on to the hope that there is a heaven to go to when we die. But what if there is no heaven and no guarantee of rebirth? What is it that we hope will continue after we die?

The idea that the self is fixed and unchanging and that the body and the ego are one and the same is an illusion. What is this entity that we are defending? For example, when you feel hurt at something someone says to you, who and what is hurt? The ego reacts, but it is a constructed image built up over time, based on your responses, perceptions, feelings, thoughts, attitudes, values and beliefs.

The ego is desperately afraid of death and tries to fight it, but ultimately the self cannot be defended. There is absolutely no way of protecting yourself from being hurt, and when we really recognize this, it brings a great sense of liberation. The more people you know, the more likely it is that there will be some of them who dislike you and who will be against you in some way. Avoiding hurt is only possible through being aggressive toward other people or oneself. You might say that *this was me for many years* the reason people do not like you is because you are not good enough or because you have something wrong with you. This only hurts yourself. Or you might like someone but are afraid that the person may not return this feeling toward you, and you do not even express what you feel for that person.

In dealing with all of this we use up around 50–60 percent of our energy. The body-mind consists of the past and fast feelings, which demands action and therefore an input of adrenaline. How do we deal with this addiction? We need our ego on the biological and psychobiological consciousness level to deal with everyday life, and there is nothing wrong with having opinions, ideas, interpretations or judgments. None of this works on the psychospiritual level, however.

If someone does not like your body, that person is telling you something about themselves and their taste, not about you. If you identify your body, your knowledge or your ideas with yourself, then you are lost. The ego is just one part of who you are. Love, for example, has nothing to do with the ego. Everything to do with the ego can be learned, trained, and exercised and is part of experience or the past. Love can never be learned or practiced, nor can dying. Dying does not belong to the ego because it is unknowable. We need to differentiate between the various states of existence to see that the instrument of the ego is effective on the biological level, but on the psychospiritual level it is a disaster.

Levels of consciousness

What is the difference between biological consciousness and psychospiritual consciousness? Biological consciousness and part of the psychological consciousness are linked closely to the genetic structure, which has to do with survival. Biological consciousness is solely concerned with survival. Without this essential mechanism, humankind would have died out long ago. Love, happiness and spirituality are not necessary for survival. The psychospiritual level is a luxury level of existence that increases the quality of life, not the quantity. Not only the spiritual teachings but also modern scientific research into the brain show that in certain states of mind it is possible to experience an expansion of consciousness.

What we need to do now is to learn to use this potential in practical terms, to look at how we actually function. According to modern physics the body is made up of atoms, and an atom is mainly composed of empty space. But even if the body is mostly emptiness and the ego is an illusion, what you feel is very real, and this does not help much when you hit your head because it still hurts. We have to distinguish between the different levels of consciousness.

The psychospiritual level has nothing to do with survival, and the ego has nothing to do with the qualities. The body exists as form with an inside, an outside and a boundary; the ego associates with the body and sees itself as form too. It therefore has the illusion that it can protect itself, defend itself and create boundaries, but it is all structured in time and duality. The ego is and always will be a prison and it can only be transformed on the psychospiritual level. Only when we see that there is something beyond duality do we find ourselves free.

Addiction to images

Psychologically we are addicted to images, or pictures of how we should be that we modify over time as our experience and knowledge increase. Ten years ago the picture you had of yourself, for example, is probably very different from the one you have now. We all see and experience things not as they truly are but distorted according to our image, our perception of the happening. The ego is totally dependent on images, and these images are in fact the substance of the ego.

The ego breathes images. And the images are reinforced all the time by adrenaline. The more fear you have, the more you will create images in your mind. The more adrenaline you need, the more you are ruled by images. This is why one of the first sentences in the Bible is about not creating images; it is why Hindu and Buddhist teachings warn us to be aware of illusion and the role of images in the process of attachment.

Most of our thoughts and ideas are so strongly conditioned that even the same words can mean different things. For example, if you say you love someone, do you mean making love, which has to do with pleasure, fulfillment and joy, or do you mean that you like and care for someone? Or if you feel sad, do you mean that you feel sorry for yourself or feel pity for someone else?

If you read one of the many books available nowadays about chakras or energy centers, you may begin to believe that they exist and that the solar plexus region is the emotional chakra. You may read somewhere else that the solar chakra has to do with fear, not the emotions. What are you going to do now? Your ego has now formed the idea that the solar plexus is the emotional chakra. Then I come along and say that chakras are not important because the Christian mystics got enlightened without knowing about them and that the emotional chakra is actually the throat area.

It is very easy to become attached to an idea that creates a form of security; then we either have to defend it against alternative ideas or we drop the original idea for the new one. This is how ideology in its extreme form becomes fascism, the belief that we are right and someone else is wrong. The worst form of fascism is spiritual fascism. So freedom is impossible if we are attached to images, ideas and a fixed notion of how things should be. We are so watchful of how we should be, how we should behave toward other people etc. All of this stops us from seeing the beauty around us. We are imprisoned by whatever is happening. To have the energy to keep yourself in this prison, you need adrenaline. Every movement of production of adrenaline on the biological consciousness level is necessary and acceptable, as it is a survival mechanism. But if you extrapolate this survival mechanism to the psychospiritual level, you create problems.

The ego is a constant defense mechanism, fighting to preserve its ideas, images, ideologies and pictures of how things should be. To be free you have to cut the past, the ego. You have to free yourself from the poisoning effects of adrenaline and from the constant desire to defend who you think you are.

Freedom from ideas

Freedom does not come from changing our ideas, beliefs or attitudes; freedom comes when we integrate everything, when we acknowledge everything without judgment or when we see through what seems to be happening to how things really are.

The action of defending something creates a separation between what is good and what is bad within you, between what is there and what you still have to achieve or to change, but there is in fact nothing to change. Change yourself and it will still be the same – only the content will be different. The best way to give your ego more power is by repeatedly saying that you have to change or be different in some way, to fulfill an ambition or to become a better person – even this, the Buddha taught, is a form of desire and craving leading to attachment and suffering.

Freedom comes when on a psychospiritual level there are no more images or ideas. In this sense, science is more spiritual than most of the esoteric movements because a serious scientist does not cling to what is known or what has already been discovered; the aim is to observe. For us, however, it is tremendously risky to live without images, ideas and ideology or as the Buddha said, "to not be attached to the idea that there is something which is you" – essentially, to be able to live without the idea of the ego. Society clings to the established, the known and to history as a form of security, but freedom only comes when there is no security at all.

What works on the biological consciousness level is not right for psychospiritual consciousness. Security is a hindrance in terms of psychospiritual consciousness because it actually blocks consciousness. The ego, the image, the idea forms this isolation. If you are a Christian and believe that salvation will come through Jesus, who is your savior, you run the risk of isolating yourself from people whose beliefs or religious practice differ from yours. This means that the isolation is not only between you and me, between you and someone else; it also creates an isolation between the idealized you and what you really are.

The moment you start to observe yourself and the things that you do not like in yourself, you create a split and therefore a conflict and confusion between the observer and the observed, between the process of desiring change and the process of judging whether or not it has happened. Whoever is watching the weakness is the weakness itself, and it is exactly this conflict that creates the problem, not the weakness as such.

The moment you focus on what is not good in you, you need to have someone observing this, which creates separation and isolation. Once you create isolation, there is automatically guilt, which arises out of fear. The moment there is guilt you are bound to react with aggression and turn this aggression toward yourself, if you are acting from an inner moralistic standpoint, or toward someone else. You might feel you have not acted according to someone else's idea of what should have been done, and ideas, an ideology, another person, or a part of one's own ego can act as the authority here.

If you feel aggression toward yourself, you blame yourself for that in you that is not good enough or needs to be changed. You then begin to watch yourself and in so doing confirm the presence of your weaknesses. This results in an increase of guilt, self-blame and constant self-questioning. The question "Why?" always leads you to a source, to someone or something to blame, which will increase the guilt even more. This in turn creates further separation and further isolation. You end up convincing yourself even more that you are the way you are because of your past. You create a cause-and-effect structure; you give the ego greater dominance and more individuality due to its particular history. The prison bars have only been strengthened, not loosened.

Stepping out of history

Ultimately it is not possible to see our weaknesses as individual to our personality. There is no weakness that is not associated with a quality. There is no weakness that is not an expression of being human. All weaknesses are impersonal; they exist all over the world and in every culture independent of belief systems and education. This is why it is so important for us to depersonalize our problems. Whatever weakness we may have, whatever name we may give it, we have a choice to trace it back to our individual history, which will then increase our isolation, guilt and aggression (remember that all of these things are a symptom of fear), or we can train our mind to see that all of these processes are part and parcel of being human. Here is the possibility for our whole psychological insight to shift. The question is no longer "Who is to blame?" or "What is the cause?" The question becomes "What are these processes?"

If we persist in believing that whatever happens to us is caused by something or someone, we will keep going, as the Buddha said, around in the endless cycle of birth and rebirth. We need to step out of the cause-and-effect pattern and begin the process of severing the past in order to free ourselves from the demands of the ego that are preoccupied with whether or not we are hurt or loved, contented or frustrated, happy or unhappy – from all the demands of expectations, hopes, duties and obligations. Then we don't have to do or say anything that is not authentic. This is what the Buddha meant by being free of identification. Remember that each form of identification is bound to bring isolation because it involves having to defend and justify. This simply creates conflict, not dissimilar to the conflict that occurs within yourself between the weakness and the observer who is observing the weakness, between good and bad. Who is it that is going to decide what is good and what is bad?

It is important here to be clear that we are not trying to get rid of the ego or to *let go* of any part of ourselves. It is a question of *letting be*, of not interfering and not creating any individual history. There is no I seeking or waiting for freedom. The I is the prison. So the question we are left with is: What is the way out if I cannot blame my history for how I am?

Three keys to freedom

The first key to helping oneself without creating conflict is related to responsibility. You might think responsibility relates to duty, but true responsibility means the ability to respond. Can you respond to the past? Can you respond to the future? Or can you respond only to what is there?

To respond to whatever is there, which is never the past or the future, is to behave responsibly. Say, for example, that you have a rational and good reason to be jealous or angry. Every feeling of jealousy is a flower of aggression and therefore a symptom of fear. Now let us say that you get angry with good reason. There are three ways in which to respond. The first, which is not connected with *responding* in the true sense of responsibility, would be to find out why you are angry. In doing this you would be moving your energy to your past. Therefore, 50 percent of the possibility for you to respond responsibly would be diverted. The second response would be to project the anger, which means taking out the anger or the jealousy on someone else. Every projection is an act of assigning the displaced aggression to the future. If you act out an emotion in this way, you may feel relieved afterward, but this is just a release of adrenaline. The result of this aggressive reaction stays in your aura system for one to two weeks and ends up disrupting your own system. Ultimately it hurts no one but yourself.

Jesus said, "If someone hits you on the left cheek, offer the right." This is a beautiful symbol for what we are talking about – forgiving also means to have no reaction. Every act of aggression has an impact on you. This doesn't come about as a result of any moral law or because of any karmic considerations but simply because you destroy your own energy system concomitantly. Any reaction at all intrinsically implies and carries with it an effect within you. To project it into the future is to block your energy.

2.

The third and the most valuable response would be not to displace this anger toward the past or the future so that all your energy is available to deal with the fast feelings as they occur. In this scenario it is possible to see the rage as it arises. If you are totally at one with the anger, it will dissolve. Where has it gone? It has only gone to where it came from, and it came from fear. *— just as our spirit returns to where it came from.*

To know yourself therefore is not simply to sit in meditation and think a little about who you are. It is about directly observing how you respond moment by moment. To respond without moving into the past or the future is the movement of love. When you feel love, it is not a romantic feeling; it is when you stop handing responsibility for how you are over to someone else.

This does not mean that you have to stop having opinions. It does not mean that you will never get angry when someone says something that may be hurtful. It does mean that you put an end to reacting to everything that may be happening around you. When this happens you may find people remarking on how they continue to feel loved by you even when they do something to hurt you. This is what it means to respond with responsibility. It is about seeing beyond the person. If you can function in this way, then you are already more or less in freedom.

The root of understanding

The second key has to do with understanding. Again, this is a paradox, as the cognitive brain is less help on the psychospiritual level. It is not about understanding in the sense of analyzing something, which means breaking something down into pieces and then creating a logical cause-and-effect structure. The root of understanding is entirely different, and if you look it up in one of the old dictionaries, you will find that the root of the word *understand* comes from the word *standing*.

Let us say that your neighbor asks you to take care of her plants while she is away on a long holiday, even though you have not the slightest idea about how to care for plants. The first thing you have to do is respond. If you agree to help her, then you have in effect taken the responsibility – you have responded to her request. By responding, you immediately create within you an interest in plants. Once you have created an interest in something, you begin the process of understanding it. You have developed a relationship to it, and you are literally *standing up* for it.

Or imagine that you start to respond to your own energy without going into the past or the future. You just feel, see, are aware of what is happening, and you discover that your heart chakra is not something that can be developed; it is always there, full of readiness to respond. You realize that how it is expressed in your daily life is only a question of how you bring the heart into what you are doing. Then someone says that you have to learn to develop and open your heart chakra. If you are to respond to this in a healthy way, having begun to understand the need to *stand up* for what you see, hear and feel, then you do not say to the person that they are wrong, that a chakra does not need to be developed. You just leave the other person in freedom to say and believe in whatever they want. You would only give your opinion if asked to.

So to understand, or to stand up for what you see, feel or realize, means that you only act out of what you yourself at that moment can be aware of, bearing in mind your limitations. In this way you do not need any ideas or knowledge to make connections on the psychospiritual level – here things cannot be understood in the same way as, for instance, we try to understand the human body. The same process occurs with love. You can study as much about love as you want, but it will not really help you become more loving. However, by responding to something, you can stand up for love, and suddenly you come to know about love.

Understanding in this sense is a feeling process, not an intellectual one. Feeling happens when a thought becomes active. Every thought creates a feeling, and when you are aware of this before it manifests on the level of the body, it is a feeling. If you wait for thought to manifest on the body level before acknowledging its existence, then it is no longer a feeling; it turns into an emotion. Calmness involves having immediate awareness of whatever is happening around you before it is structured on the level of the body as an emotion. It is very important not to allow things to manifest on the level of the body. In relation to spiritual practice, we hear a lot about being the master of the body, letting go of the body or getting out of the body.

[handwritten margin notes: "Emotion", "the 'feeling travels to the Body..."]

The divisions between philosophy, psychology and neuroscience center around the question of duality between body, mind, soul or oneness. Some people are fascinated by past lives, despite the fact that it is all about accumulating more history. The way to freedom is to get out of history. Freedom comes when we understand how to cut through the accumulation of images and therefore the history and isolation that follow – to step out of our cause-and-effect structure, out of our time-limited ego, out of the endless cycle of birth and rebirth. Then we have the first glimpse of oneness and beauty and begin to see the beauty of other people.

Trust and surrender

The third key is trust. Going back to our previous example, if you respond to your neighbor and take on the responsibility of caring for the plants, then simply by accepting that responsibility, you automatically begin to have a better understanding of plants. Trust follows whenever we stand up for anything that we are in relationship with. If your neighbor calls you later and says she forgot to mention some other plants in an upstairs room, then through the trust and understanding you have built up, you will be able to take on more responsibility.

Through responsibility you understand more, through understanding you develop more trust and through trust, you have more responsibility. We can start with responsibility, understanding or trust. For the Christian mystics it was trust, for the Hindus it was understanding and for the Buddhists it was responsibility. It does not matter where you start, as they all feed into each other. What does the mind (or the ego) do if there is insecurity? It immediately clings to the known, which is the past. It attaches itself to something familiar. Trust means that we detach from the past. It is about not sticking to what we know. Wisdom never comes from clinging to knowledge; it comes through opening up to what is not known. This can only happen through trust, or what in Buddhism is known as surrender. Again, we need to be careful what is meant here.

As the Buddha said, above all, don't believe what I say; examine it and if it fits with your own experience, so be it. Surrender really means to give greater value to the unknown than the known. Surrender, according to the Christian mystics, essentially means to trust, but it is not about trusting in a person or an idea, although this happens automatically when we stop dealing in images.

We are all frightened of falling in love and being in love because love cannot be controlled – it is the unknown; it is unpredictable. Aggression, on the other hand, is predictable – we can act upon our aggression. Love is totally unpredictable, and if we open ourselves up to whatever might happen, there are no guarantees, and we allow ourselves to become vulnerable. To trust is to open up totally, and in doing so we will sometimes be dealing with people who may take advantage of us. It is better to be cheated by another than to cheat oneself, however, because being cheated by others does not hurt us energetically.

Cheating yourself will hurt you because it involves images, the ego, emotions and our own individual isolation. Bear in mind here that when a situation arises where we are cheated in life, or feel that we are, it is not necessarily about karma or punishment in response to a previous cause.

Even in surrender the ego is still present because we need it in order to function on the biological and the psychobiological consciousness level. Without it we would be unable to live our lives; it has its own value, and it does not interfere with psychospiritual processes. And when these three keys – responsibility, understanding and trust – are working together, there is total, absolute freedom.

CHAPTER 9

Relationship, Consciousness and Love

When we are able to be in relationship with responsibility, understanding and trust, we experience the freedom of interconnection, which affects how we are in the outside world; we feel more open, there is a sense of equanimity and potential, we see how relationship is our natural way of being. As soon as we experience conflict and tension in a relationship, however, we tend to think we have to analyze it and somehow come up with a way to "work through it." Most of us who go into therapy do so because of relationship problems, and we find that ultimately the real "problem" is that we don't know how to relate to ourselves or even who is doing the relating and to what.

Consciousness and meditation

In an attempt to improve the quality of life, many people are interested in practicing meditation – but what do we mean by meditation? There are two main forms of meditation and various techniques we can try out. We can aim to calm the mind, quiet the thoughts and aim for transcendence or we can practice a form of meditation in which we simply observe how we are and gradually create a better relationship with ourselves.

The absence of the associative thought process, which brings in the past and the future, is the most effective form of meditation for us if we want to improve how we relate to ourselves and others. Here the awareness is directed toward *being empty*, and through this we arrive at a state of being. Where do thoughts come from? It is easy to observe the beginning of a thought, the movement through the thought and the ending of the thought. Thought is always a description of something. Thought originates from consciousness. Thoughts are what we call the flowers of consciousness. Consciousness does not originate from the brain; it is a chain of observation that is transmitted through the brain in the same way that transmissions reach a television screen. The quality aura is a part of consciousness.

Thought originates out of consciousness, so it cannot come from anywhere other than the potential, the qualities. Thought originates from consciousness, and consciousness is part of the quality aura. Truly seeing this will have a tremendous impact on your whole being. It means that whatever you do is initiated by a thought, a thought being a description. It means that we always have this trace and that whatever we do comes out of thinking. Consciousness will always contain a memory of whatever you have done, not in a structure of punishment and reward but merely as a part of the whole of consciousness. Whatever step you take in your endeavors will contribute to the atmosphere of consciousness. This simply means that your actions form part of the whole influence of consciousness.

What consequences does this have? It means that the unknown, and the fear toward the unknown, can only be resolved through contact with our qualities. One suddenly begins to understand why mystics emphasize meditation. Meditation is not the absence of thought – it is the realization that thoughts are the individual flowers of consciousness and that in trying to understand our human processes one has to deal not with the thoughts but instead with consciousness itself. The description provided by thoughts can be a thing of beauty, but it is never the complete reality. Meditation is simply the movement of letting the quality part of consciousness become more dominant than the description.

Movement in stillness

No amount of knowledge, no interpretation, no description or logical understanding can ever free anyone. It is only movement within stillness that creates freedom. The mind, however, perceives stillness as something dangerous and lives in the illusion of representing reality. Stillness creates an openness that enables us to see that there is not just one reality. This shatters the mind's security, so what can we do if only stillness can free the mind and yet the mind is afraid of stillness? The mind cannot command itself to relax and not be afraid of stillness. Doing this is bound to make it react with fear because stillness shatters its security. Whenever insecurity comes in, even if only for a second, the mind will immediately try to find a thousand ways to build up security.

There are various processes for building up security – for example, we can subscribe to belief systems, concepts and ideologies, or we can say that there is no value in stillness as it is only through thinking, reflecting and analyzing that we can learn. The mind claims that stillness is nothing – but observe the beauty of the word *nothing*. No thing. Whatever the mind does, it is always creating a *thing*. Stillness is no thing. Believing is not living out that which one believes in; the act of believing is a means of holding ideas within the mind. Stillness takes all of this away.

If you meditate using a specific technique, you simply do not meditate. You create a belief in something and your mind is meditating according to a certain technique. Even in our sleep, there is no stillness. Dreams do nothing more than show that, even in sleep, there is no stillness. The brain could easily function, even during sleep, without registering all the discharge of chemical reactions that we call dreams. We are so insecure that we even have to interpret dreams, but they are not the full picture.

The motivative thought process is a constant movement toward something, in contrast with the associative thought process. When sitting in meditation, which is movement with stillness occurring concurrently, we can only sit there without the slightest interaction or interpretation, conclusion or identification if the motivative thought process is active. It is as if the associative thought process is the car, while the motivative thought process is the driver. Or imagine a tightrope walker centered in stillness. The center is stillness.

This requires less focusing on goals and not overactivating the associative thought process. The motivative thought process can just take the lead and guide. The spiritual word *guidance* does not, by the way, mean being dependent on someone or something – it comes from the movement of being in a steady flow simply through stillness and without wanting to achieve anything. A river, for example, flows steadily from the mountain to the ocean, but it has no awareness when it starts in the mountain that it will end in the ocean. It is just flowing. On the other hand, if you are too relaxed, the chances are you might fall asleep or the mind might get so involved in fantasy that you forget what you are doing.

Total harmony or balance is achieved through being poised in what is in-between, and this state of being in the in-between can only happen through the motivative thought process. The motivation here is not to reach anything, remember. When viewed in this way, the tightrope walker suddenly has elegance. The process also begins to look easy. Whenever there is too much focusing or insufficient focus, and whenever there is too much motivation to achieve something, then elegance gets lost. Try to be in love and you will only end up being terribly tense. Try to reach love and the act of trying, as such, will prevent love. The motivation is just to be there, centered in stillness like the tightrope walker and to move slightly forward.

The same process occurs within the body in the immune system. The body can be a tremendous learning tool for the mind. If the immune system is too active, it will overreact. If it is not active enough, then we become prone to different kinds of illnesses. A healthily functioning immune system is in fact the perfect tightrope walker. One can always learn from the body, but one is not just the body; likewise, one can always learn from the mind or the aura, but one is not just the mind or the aura.

When no attitude of meditation is present, we either identify with the body, the mind or the aura system. The tightrope walker cannot identify with the foot he is putting down because he immediately has to move the other foot. He cannot identify with his arms being outstretched; he just needs to move, to flow, while having an awareness of every reaction, sensation and movement that is present.

If you start to move toward asking what the process of thought is, which immediately includes everybody and everything in your observation, then the possibilities exist for you to be a part of consciousness. If you shift from the content of thoughts to the observation of the process of thoughts, then you suddenly find that you do not need to fight or to justify from the perspective of personality. We cannot separate stillness and depersonalization. Whenever there is movement without stillness, no matter what happens, we act out of our sense of self. Stillness creates space. Without stillness we cannot be in the movement of investigating thought.

Stillness and movement

To begin to look at ourselves and how we are in the world then, we need to learn stillness – not just the stillness of meditation practice but also in our everyday lives. Just taking a few moments to go outside and look at the sky in the evening can bring us into stillness where we can be in touch with our true consciousness and the quality aura. If we feel lost, confused or stuck, for example, and connect to our wider consciousness, we will be contacting guidance through the quality aura, which is the atmosphere of the soul. This involves movement in stillness, so the associative thought processes are not running. If you find yourself beginning to look for words to describe it, you are back in thought. Just let the thought pass gently, and observe what happens.

The observer who observes that Timeless observer is not a part of you; it is that which survives you. The "you" is the body, the mind and the aura. The observer may be connected somehow with the quality aura. The soul may have a connection to the observer observing the Timeless observer, but it has absolutely no personality. Whenever you are in touch with the observer observing the Timeless observer, then you are in touch with the world.

Krishnamurti put it beautifully when he said, "We are the world." When we are in touch with the observer we are not only in touch with others, we are in touch with everything that has been and will be. We realize that our own beauty, our own weaknesses, are a part of everyone else's, without the need for moral or theoretical structures. Out of this awareness comes humbleness and compassion. The process of depersonalization and meditation, which is directionless movement in stillness away from your personality, brings us into relationship with the observer – with universal consciousness, the Creator, God, the Tao or whatever you want to call it. This is what is meant by spirituality.

Love and creativity

The essence or the medium in which our qualities exist is love. It is our nature to love. My son Fabian, for example, is loving because he is already aware of the nature of love; he is the experience of love, and the more I love him the more he will appreciate it because he will be free to continue giving love and receiving love. The act of waiting for love before being able to express it means that your qualities are being imprisoned.

Imagine a painting of a rural landscape with fields, trees, maybe a stream, and within that picture you can also see an angel. There is also a house that looks dilapidated from lack of care and that now has to be renovated. This house represents all your problems and weaknesses –

your rebellious qualities. So the painting includes at the same time the neglected house, the picturesque countryside and the angel. When you study the picture, how much does it matter to know exactly when the artist painted a particular aspect of it and with which color? Is it not more important just to look at the whole picture?

It is exactly the same with the qualities. You have a responsibility toward yourself to express your qualities, and, like a work of art, the moment something is finished, it no longer needs your attention. The love is in the actual creation with its imperfection. The finished picture is not a prerequisite for the life of the artist; he is not living through the finished painting. He may be dependent on what it can bring him from a material point of view, but his qualities are expressed through the act of creating the painting, not from the results.

Looking at the whole picture without bringing time into it takes you away from the wholeness, the oneness of it. Watch the whole picture, and understanding will come through being totally absorbed in the whole, not by a preoccupation with knowing which part was created and when. Watch how the mind thinks that knowing just how the picture was created will bring about understanding. From the perspective of the energy body, the mind provides an insight into part of the picture, but this partial understanding will not include a feeling and understanding for the whole.

Seeing the whole picture

You as an energy body are already limited by gravity, space and time. It is possible to live in this way, but the danger is that we limit ourselves even further to the point where the presence of the energy body can no longer be seen or felt. The artist who painted the picture would probably not be able to tell you which color he started with or in which order he painted the picture. He would probably say that he has no cause-and-effect relationship with it. Picasso, for example, said in reply to a question as to which painting of his he liked the most:

"What a question! The one I am working on is the one I like most. If I were to like one of the others more than this I would not be able to paint." He used to get depressed when he was not painting, a signal that he was not in the process of using his qualities.

Relationship can only be created to whatever I am involved in now, to that which is not yet finished. Once it is finished it is gone, released. When our qualities are limited by coming into gravity, or being born, there is no need for us to learn anything; it is not an indication of the lack of anything. It is simply an unfinished picture. Until then not only are you not whole but everything is not one.

The question is not how much love you get; it is how much love you give. If you feel someone loves you, you must already have some idea about love. To be able to entertain the idea of love you need first to feel loving, to experience giving love. When someone does not love you, behind the fear that you are not loved, when you go to the root of how you feel, you are actually sad that you are not being given the opportunity to love; you are robbed of the opportunity to express the gift of love. You are sad simply because you feel you are not being allowed to give, to move outward with your love.

The moment you try to perfect yourself, you stop the relationship to your qualities. Love exists in the state of imperfection, and if you look for perfection you destroy love. The Christian mystics called this humbleness or humility. There is no need for perfection; there is only a need to look at problems and weaknesses and see how they are signals that you are not really letting your qualities work. If you believe that your past, your history, your childhood is the cause of what you are now, then your memory of what happened to you is influenced by that belief.

This means our life is much less conditioned and influenced by our actual childhood than it is influenced by the images, the memory and the pictures that we have about it all. We are less psychologically damaged by our actual childhood than by the traumatic way in which we remember it. If again you take the example of the picture of the angel, the dilapidated house and the countryside, and if you believe that you only have to put the house in order to become whole, then you will not see the angel. You will only see the house and what you need to do to it, which brings you back to cause and effect.

The activity and process of creating is a movement with and toward something. The qualities always work through the atmosphere of living or the actuality of being. As a result of this mixture, for example, in painting a picture, more and more of it becomes the whole, but if you limit it to time, cause-and-effect, there is no mixture – there is no melting between the quality and the actual doing. The whole, the oneness, is not in any way mystical – it is simply the movement of the quality combining with the doing and through this process creating oneness.

Plato referred to *evdaemonia*, a Greek word that means a happy soul. Just as a heart-to-heart connection allows us to appreciate the people we love just as they are, a soul connection opens us to a further dimension. We then see the possibilities of our relationship in terms of who they could be and who we could become under their influence. When we love someone, if we have a heart connection, this relates to physical and mental levels of consciousness. Conflicts at the heart level result in arguments about character. If we have a soul connection it relates to the potential for our qualities to manifest through love. On the soul level there are no conflicts, and the qualities are supported.

Friendship is based on soul connections where one deals with and supports the qualities, yet there need not be a physical or sexual connection. And for a relationship to be lasting and fulfillling, it is not enough to be able to relate just on the sexual and heart energy level. The soul level connection also needs to be there in order for the qualities to be supported. That is also why friendship and having a good network of social friends is so very important.

Love and sadness

While love is the vehicle that carries the qualities, they may or may not be manifest when love is present. You can love your partner, but it is still not a guarantee that the qualities are coming through. The qualities are repressed not through some specific personal action – in spite of loving and of being loved, there may be no connection to your own qualities, to the energy body, the soul consciousness. The only way to bring about change is to break the pattern, whatever it might be, so that it does not continue – to go back to the source, to get in touch again with your energy body, which houses the qualities.

In the process of moving toward stillness and forgetting the demands of the ego for a while, there is expansion and the possibility to experience a broadening of one's boundaries. Our bodies relax and we feel less defended psychologically. We are in a state where we can be touched by something. Basically, we are all addicted to touch, be it physically or psychological, because it releases the neurotransmitter serotonin in the brain.

Staying with this flow of love becomes difficult over time as the mind develops and grows. The processes of the mind are in sympathy with biopsychological consciousness but do not sit quite so comfortably with psychospiritual consciousness. To stay connected to the source of love, we need to stay connected to our feelings of sadness. Sadness is the bridge to love. Sometimes when you are in a state of sadness you will find yourself in a situation where there is absolutely no possibility of escape.

If someone close to you is dying, for example, shortly before they die you may feel self-pity. You are in grief because the person is leaving you, and you are also afraid about what you are going to do when you are left alone. Now imagine that there is absolutely no more hope of a recovery and that the person is definitely going to die. At this point it would be rather cruel to continue to say to the dying person, "You are not going to die, you will get better." If you can be totally with the person who is dying, then you will experience a complete change of feeling. There will be sadness, and at the same time there will be a tremendous surge of energy, which is neither bliss nor joy. You find yourself in a state where you know that there is absolutely nothing that you can do for or against the situation, and it is this state that the mystics called the *dying of the ego*.

When you are totally with something, without any recourse to escape or excuses, you drop into sadness. And this sadness marks the ending of your history, and the way to love. Love is at the beginning, not at the end of your history. Love is the flowering of the ending. Before you can die metaphorically (remember that the dying process is the process of sadness) you have to be in a state where there is absolutely no running away from your problems or weaknesses. The key is total awareness and not just acceptance of what is in front of you, a direct observation of whatever is present and what the process is.

Moving toward love
Love is exactly the same movement as sadness. It is something you cannot summon up, nor avoid when it happens. You cannot manipulate it. It seems that people are more afraid of love than of being criticized. Love destroys the ego even more than sadness. A passage from *A Course In Miracles* says: "There is only light. Light here is a symbol for love. When human beings move toward this light, the fear actually becomes greater. It is not our differences, nor our problems which really create fear. It is the light that does." Or, in the words of Carl Gustav Jung, "The most fearful thing for man is to become complete." Being complete means being like everyone else and not identifying with one's own likes and dislikes, knowledge, attitudes, beliefs and everything we construct to build up our sense of self.

Sadness is part of the dying process of the ego. Compassion, which is love in combination with sadness, is constantly present in the universe, and each one of us is part of the carrier of this flame. This sadness or love is the energy body, which is made up of the quality aura and the soul. We can call the quality aura the atmosphere of the soul without needing to know exactly what the soul is but recognizing that it is a higher vibration, not in the sense of value but higher in frequency. It is a natural law that higher vibrations or higher levels of energy always penetrate lower levels and never the other way around.

Weaknesses have a lower vibrational frequency. At the beginning of life there is a tremendous collection of high frequency vibration; later on the body-mind appears. We cannot hope to reach a higher vibration via the body, but higher energy can subtly penetrate through lower energy. The spirit is in the body, but it is not the body.

Activating the qualities

How long are we willing to fight with shadows? For example, Paul struggled against Jesus and his teachings, then suddenly on his way to Damascus he experienced enlightenment and transformation. Enlightenment is an accident. If we are to carry this energy or the flame throughout our lives, it is natural for it to try by every means available to shine through in any form of expression until it can be in total expression. Therefore, all psychological problems and weaknesses are a manifestation, a response and a signal from the body-mind to reach out and connect with the quality. Whenever the qualities, which are part of love, are not expressed, there will be a reaction or signal from the body-mind. This happens not only because of what happened in your childhood, although that may play a certain role, but mainly because if you do not use your qualities you will experience a gentle reminder to get back in touch with your qualities. We need to be able to express our qualities. When we fall in love, for example, we are able to share our love with someone, and 80 percent of our weakness and problems are suddenly gone simply because our quality structure is suddenly activated.

Each psychological problem is an attempt to get back to the quality, a symptom of not being in touch with our roots, our true nature. As the nature of each one of us is love, then love will somehow try to shine through. It is like the sun constantly trying to penetrate the clouds. It does not give up, and the higher vibration will always absorb the lower vibration. There is no energy system or bodywork that can activate love. When we are truly aware of this, the mind starts a process of inquiry. What is the weakness trying to get at, which quality does it wish to reconnect with, which part of the quality aura does it want to express?

Getting in touch with the soul

The English mystic Evelyn Underhill said, "As long as you are not in touch with the soul, there will be a tremendous fire burning in you. Even when you reach the soul, you still have this tremendous fire in you because you never know whether the soul that you think you have reached is the soul ... therefore, one has to stay totally with what is there without any escape." (*Practical Mysticism*, Ariel Press, 1987)

If we work with the lower vibrations, or our weaknesses, there is a desire to get rid of the weakness followed by the fear that we may not succeed. This fear takes away all the energy that could be used to connect with the higher vibrations that can absorb the weakness or lower vibration. Some weaknesses are direct opposites of their corresponding quality, and this depends on the whole atmosphere of the person. For example, shyness is the quality of not always thinking that you know everything, a tremendous quality, which in Christian terminology is known as humility. It has its meaning according to the specific atmosphere and personal structure of the individual and how the person is dealing with their daily life situations.

Each weakness is a manifestation, a response to try to get back in touch with the quality, so we have to try to understand (but not intellectually) what exactly this quality aura is. We need to be able to somehow observe it. That is what Buddha meant by the word *observation*. Love is the reason that your body-mind is functioning and alive. So whenever something opposed to love appears, you become alert. If you had not originated out of love, then you could not possibly be alerted to any weakness. The weaknesses just would not matter. To even be aware of your weakness means that your foundation is love. The fact that we are aware of our weaknesses is proof in itself of the presence of the energy body or quality aura.

The courage of presence

We need to have the courage to do what Jesus, Buddha, Krishna and all the great mystics have said: to be totally present, to just observe whatever is there and to create a relationship to it. Relationship is the movement of love. Whenever you choose to work with the lower vibrations, you create a distance. Love is the total absence of distance. Absence of distance is enlightenment. Every weakness is a desperate search of the body-mind to again be in a relationship with the soul or the quality aura – to regain the ability to radiate the light of love.

Love and consciousness are not the same. Consciousness is created through love; love is not created through more consciousness. Therefore, whatever you do in your work, you cannot create love. If love were energy, then by creating a very strong flow of energy, love would exist, but in reality this does not happen. More consciousness is not a guarantee of more love, but love is a guarantee of more consciousness.

The process of love

Consciousness goes together with understanding. Whenever you try to understand something, you limit the movement of love. You cannot understand love. You can love another person, but the moment you try to understand them, you limit love. The moment you try to understand a weakness, you take the movement of love away from the problem, and so the higher vibration cannot absorb it. You can accumulate as much consciousness as you want, but it will not bring more love into your being. The truth is that love does not require any prerequisite for it to exist. It is unconditional. When the mind sees this process, real relaxation happens for the first time. Things just fall into place. It is not a process of letting go; who is going to let go? There is no desire to resist or to want to be different; it is the Buddha's *tathata*, which simply means *it is as it is*.

Exactly in this moment of sadness, the quality aura, the higher vibration, can start to move through the body-mind, and there is transformation into love. Love does not require any effort. One of the biggest misunderstandings is that you first have to receive love before you can love yourself and others. To love yourself is in fact the movement of loving others, because whenever you love someone else, you realize that there is very little difference between you and anyone else. Suddenly, you find that through loving others you love yourself because you realize it is the same process of inner expression.

Whatever is there, just totally observe it. Do not ask why, do not ask whether you like it, do not ask whether it would be helpful or not. Simply step out of time. Whatever comes up, just be in touch with it. Whenever you are in touch with it, whatever is there, even if it seems unbearable, there will be love. Whenever there is love, you have transformation.

Inner expression is about observing and sharing with yourself in the first instance. Observing something and staying with it is the process of love. The mystics knew that love is the movement away from oneself. If the movement is too much toward ourselves, it turns into narcissism or self-love, which is destructive. Moving away from oneself really means moving away from body-mind toward the energy body, seeing the body-mind for what it is, a beautiful instrument that has a purpose. The purpose is to carry the flame, or the energy body and the soul.

First we see our body-mind, which has a beginning and an end and is therefore structured in time or duality, then we see something that is not structured in time – love. Sadness is the bridge from duality to nonduality. Love is the atmosphere in which this movement takes place.

CHAPTER 10

From Fear to Sadness

However we might feel about our lives, whatever we might think about our capabilities or intelligence, these feelings of bliss, love and joy are totally independent of who we are. Getting into a state of bliss is just a question of whether we can cross the bridge from duality to nonduality, and the ability to do this is absolutely and totally independent of knowledge. All the slow feelings are not dependent on our efforts or on our intellectual understanding. This is why we fall in love with all our weaknesses intact; this is why while out walking in the countryside we can suddenly experience a feeling of bliss.

Our society is based on a competition and comparing process, even when it comes to spirituality. The only thing we need is ourselves, just as we are with our weaknesses and qualities. Love, bliss and joy have nothing to do with competition or comparing. So the first thing to remember is that you need nothing other than what you already have in order to cross the bridge of sadness to love.

The courage to cross
Why then is it so difficult to cross this bridge? If I can be happy even with all my weaknesses, why is this so difficult to do? The mind, of course, will persist in trying to understand, but again it has nothing to

do with understanding. Go down this route and we are once again in the trap of knowledge, learning, achieving and competition.

The only thing we really have to deal with is the fear of not being loved – which is really the sadness at not being given the opportunity to express or demonstrate love, to share it, to bring out and manifest your potential, your qualities. Whenever we move away from knowledge or from the known, fear is naturally present. Once we see this, then suddenly fear is no longer an enemy. Instead, it is the first signal that we are really growing, that we are really moving away from attachment.

The Buddha said – in a very beautiful statement, which many Buddhists try to avoid dealing with – that it is quite easy to be detached from material things, but it is a little more difficult to be detached from our belief systems, from our thoughts, from our inside pictures.

The real step out of the wheel of birth and rebirth is when we are detached from our own consciousness. This is in complete contrast to everything we hear about how we have to gain consciousness of ourselves, and it takes courage to face stepping out of it.

Detachment and growth

To be detached from consciousness is to question our very being, to threaten our very existence. This automatically brings fear, which always means leaving behind what we know; it is the process of moving toward the unknown. To detach from our consciousness would mean enlightenment, to become transformed, for example, as experienced by Paul on the road to Damascus. The Buddha said it in another way. He said: have absolutely no identification and you will be enlightened. There is no way to become enlightened other than to be able to walk with fear. The question then is: Do you see fear as an enemy or as a signal that you are moving toward something new? There is no possibility for transformation or real growth without fear being present. If you want to avoid fear at all costs on the spiritual level, then you will never become spiritual, and you will not be able to benefit from slow feelings such as joy or bliss. When you face death you will cling to everything that you identify with, and you will not be able to die in peace because all your remaining energy will be fighting the fear instead of surrendering to the natural movement in dissolving onto the other side.

Fear is the first sign that you are in fact on the right track. When fear comes up – the signal that you are moving toward the unknown – you are really making a step out of attachment, and at this point it is vitally important not to react. When there is absolutely no reaction, there is a huge input of awareness. When you fight fear, you limit your perspective; you do not become the incisive instrument of perception that you could be. In fighting fear on the psychospiritual level, you limit yourself to what you are now. What you are now is not what you could be tomorrow.

Imagine that you are a seed; it does not matter exactly what kind of a seed you are because a seed is not conscious of what it will be. By its very nature a seed is just aware of being a seed, which is a metaphor for a potential. The seed as a seed in its form, with its consciousness of being a seed, has to die if it wants to grow to its fullest potential of being a tree, a plant or whatever. Suppose that the seed has a mind as we have, which is evolving but at the same time in conflict – there is a sense somewhere that something more is possible, but it does not know whether to stay as a seed and be secure in the knowledge it has about itself. Even with all the best of its intentions and efforts, the mind of the seed can never know what it will become. It will not even be aware of this at the moment of dying, because at the point of death, that is at the point at which it changes its form, it is no longer a seed and it therefore cannot be conscious of what it is.

It can try as hard as it wants, but it will never come to the realization that when it dies it will be a tree. It can create all the consciousness it can about itself, but it will simply be an illusion. Then one day the seed sees through the illusion and sees that the only way it can reach its potential is by allowing that transformation to happen.

Embracing the fear

If you wait until the end of your life when you physically die and your body dissolves, this will not be the real dying process that we are referring to. If you wait until then to engage in the dying process, then you have missed the point of life. You have missed experiencing your own beauty in this life.

None of us is certain when we will die; the only certainty is that it will happen, and death itself is not important. The seed's readiness to die without knowing what it will become is the crux of the matter. Moving through the process of transformation will be frightening, and the fear is the process of knowing that you are on the way to becoming your potential, even though you may not know what it will be. The only consciousness that is left just before the point of transformation is fear. If all seeds were to behave as our mind does, there would be no life on earth, and the world would have died long ago. Transformation does not happen as a result of making an effort or being especially conscious; it happens when you embrace and welcome fear. Fear is always the process, the signal that you are moving toward the unknown, the new. Do you want to stay as a seed, which is a beautiful but rather limited form, or do you want to transform?

There can be no transformation without fear. All the mystics and ancient texts provide us with information about the dark night of the soul, the vale of tears, the phase of confusion. The mind, of course, wants transformation without having to move into the unknown, like the seed wanting to immediately become a tree, but this is simply not possible, and it goes against nature.

If the mind can stop reacting to fear, suddenly the fear vanishes. It just becomes absent, and there is only awareness. You then find yourself standing on the edge of the bridge of awareness. It is known as choiceless awareness or desireless awareness – a state of being when awareness is not focused on a specific subject but is just pure awareness.

Toward awareness

What happens if you observe and you do not split consciousness into two – i.e., the person who is aware and who is observing that they are aware and the person who is this awareness?

Imagine that you are sitting in front of a huge wall with hundreds of televisions, and each television is tuned into a different program. There are hundreds of programs, and you do not see anything other than these television screens. Imagine that these televisions represent the processes of your brain. There is also no other light in the room except the light that is created by the movement on the screens. Now and then, one or more of these televisions goes off. At first you do not notice any visible difference, so if five channels are turned off there is no apparent change. There is still the same noise, still a lot of information and still a lot of light in the room.

If slowly one channel after another goes off, you will be more conscious of which programs are on. When you reach a point where there are only six televisions left on, it is very easy to be aware of all of them. You can suddenly hear the words much better, the meaning, the music, and there is less light. One more television goes off and then another one, until there is only one left. You now have a good ability to concentrate, to understand, to see, and there is still light. Now you turn off the last television. There is silence, no more input of information and no more light.

That is exactly when awareness comes in. You are suddenly totally in touch with yourself. It is dark, it is silent and there is nothing to see. That is when you might think something is wrong, and you try to switch on the screen of the mind again. If, however, you do not reactivate your thinking processes, and this usually takes two or three minutes, you will start to see light again. Darkness is only darkness until the brain gets used to it. This is awareness. Awareness, when it is not split, becomes stillness. Stillness is the absence of fear. Stillness is the first signal that you are in that which is new, where you are no longer attached to knowledge, definition, experience and history.

What happens in a state of awareness and stillness? The past and the known become absent; for the first time you may feel that you are not separate from everyone else and that you are just like all the others. All your feelings, including fast feelings, are nothing other than a natural outcome of being human as they are for everybody else. Your personal history changes the picture a little, but there are still the universal feelings such as guilt, aggression, jealousy, greed, comparing, self-pity, doubting, blaming, feeling obligated – all this is part and parcel of being human. Liberation does not mean that you rid yourself of these feelings, emotions and processes. Liberation means that you realize it has nothing to do with your personal history. This is what is meant by "dropping out of the wheel of birth and rebirth," dropping out of karma – not that you are not human, but you are no longer confined to your individual history.

This is awareness: the ability to see that all that you are is also happening every day to millions of other people irrespective of society or culture. What happens then is that you start to feel the atmosphere of sadness that is created by all of it.

marriage

The atmosphere of sadness
Sadness is not sorrow, grief or self-pity, the feeling of not being loved or accepted. Sadness is an atmosphere generated by the realization that the seed, or your history, has ended. The seed is your history, but the potential and manifestation of the seed, which is the tree, is more than individual history. Jesus gave a beautiful example in the sowing of seeds, some of which fall in the thorn bush, some fall on stony ground and some fall elsewhere. The question is not about the seed – there are millions of seeds sown every day. The question is about the manifesta-

tion of the seed into the apple tree. It makes no sense if the apple tree
would prefer to be a pear tree. It is still essentially a fruit tree, its fruit
is grown to be eaten; it is a life cycle. In the same way, our individual
manifestation, our different appearance, culture, gender, tastes and so
on do not change the overall purpose. The point is what is it for? In a
state of awareness, of stillness, where history and knowledge are absent, you realize that sadness unites all of us, giving us the feeling of
being interconnected.

It is not possible to respond to all the general misery and suffering in
the world, but with someone we know personally we would feel sadness. Imagine a friend has had a miscarriage, and you feel sad. Does
the sadness you feel for your friend give you negative feelings, make
you depressed or does it give you a feeling of closeness, a sense of
sharing? If it is really sadness you are experiencing, then it will be the
latter; the former is self-pity. Sadness gives you a feeling of strength,
which is the first step toward love. When we are really happy, we cry
the same tears as when we are sad – they cannot be separated even
biologically. In order to transform we have to detach from our personal history all the time. Thought originates from consciousness, and
consciousness is part of the quality aspect. Happiness is a state of being when consciousness and the qualities are manifesting through the
body-mind aura.

Once the seed has died, the tree can only produce fruit if it is constantly detaching itself from its "seedness" – in other words, to feel
truly alive we need to have feelings like caring, for example, which
means that we detach ourselves from ourselves; "you" are absent. The
absence of you occurs when there is stillness and awareness, and this
begins with sadness. It leaves you helpless – but in a positive sense.
Sadness, in contrast to self-pity, leaves you literally standing in stillness, feeling for the other person, and this is compassion. Sadness does
not create the need to be doing anything. It leaves you "without doing." The Chinese masters called it *wu wei* – doing in not doing –
totally being there without doing. Sadness can then move to joy.

When you go to a church or to a holy place, the stronger the overall atmosphere, the less you have an urge to act. Slow feelings are all atmospheres within which there is nonaction. Love is not a movement of action; it is a movement of just being there.

Imagine that you go to visit someone who is dying. If you are constantly trying to find ways to help, this will disturb the process. It would be better for you to just be there, not to try to let go but simply because by just being there you will cross the bridge of sadness. No reaction to fear brings you directly to awareness, through to stillness and the atmosphere that is sadness, the caring capacity, the act of totally being there, and the outcome of this is love, joy and bliss.

Once all the slow feelings and sadness move away from the past, then bliss appears from nowhere. Happiness has no cause and it is not structured in time. The ego is structured in time, but the ego in itself is not the problem – the false association made from one level of consciousness to another creates all of our difficulties. The key is to remember that we function on different levels of consciousness – out-of-body consciousness, mind/brain consciousness and surfing between the two.

Newtonian physics does not negate quantum physics, but neither are they the same. Happiness is the process of falling out of yourself, falling out of the past. The body is not afraid of dying. The mind in fact is also not afraid of dying, whether it happens tomorrow or in thirty years' time. What we do habitually is project the real fear of the unknown that is happening to everyone all the time onto the future event of our physical death.

Leaving ourselves behind

In fact, the real fear is that we have to leave behind every moment of the past, and as the mind has so much difficulty with this it cannot deal with emptiness, it projects forward and starts creating an image of what it thinks is the *real* death. At the same time, the mind can see that to project this into the future is an illusion. We cannot really be afraid of our biological death right now because we cannot fully imagine how it will be. However, the mind still clings onto this fear because it knows that this is not the real fear. The real fear is in-between this image of death and what you feel now. It is the in-between of emptiness, of not knowing, which is the real fear. So the mind clings and attaches itself to whatever it can in order to feel safe.

This is exactly what the Buddha meant by stepping out of the wheel of birth and rebirth. It is not about analyzing your past; it is about seeing the fear for what it is. We need to stop all identification, which can only ever be with the past. Jesus talked of setting ourselves free by seeing and engaging in the process of forgiveness. Death is not an ending; it is the rearranging of a structure, like the bud of a flower opening and in doing so being in constant change. The form has just rearranged itself. Our weaknesses bring us to the point of opening, the process of rearrangement, at which point we need to take the weakness, really see it and use it as a form of strength to open up to our qualities. The caterpillar becomes a butterfly through a process; evolution is a constant movement that cannot be understood – it can only be directly observed. Simply observe all that is there: strengths, qualities and weaknesses alike. If you can see the beauty in you, then you will suddenly see beauty all around you. The movement of observing this beauty is compassion.

How can we help ourselves to do this? There are some helpful guidelines to assist us in crossing over the bridge of sadness, but if you become too fixed on them (or too attached to them), you will become trapped in yet another identification. Your attachment to any model, technique or set of guidelines has to be so loose that what is new and unknown can always shine through. It is possible to break down the process – moving from fear to sadness and through stillness and awareness to love and joy – into six steps.

Learn to forget. This is the process of forgiveness. Forgiving is the process of cutting the past. Learning to forget is not about forgetting how to operate on the material level; it concerns memory on the psychospiritual level. Memory on the psychospiritual level has to fade away regularly. You need to be prepared to see, feel and listen to things anew every day. Life cannot be seen in this way if we are not always in a process of forgetting. Use memory only where it is needed. When it comes to being in touch with human beings, you do not need memory apart from being able to recognize people. The person you meet today may behave totally differently from how they were yesterday. The act of seeing things afresh can only happen if you are ready to forget your past and your history.

Learn to be awake (handwritten annotation)

Learn to be aware. Through awareness itself we become aware. Awareness brings awareness through awareness. Awareness is not about you concentrating on your consciousness; it is just fading away into stillness and comes through experiencing that which is new. That which is new only comes to you if you do not react to fear. Stillness is the absence of what is known.

Be in relationship. However you may find yourself to be at this point in time, be constantly in relationship. Make being socially active your biggest priority. There are individual relationships (or primary relationships) and social relationships. Individual relationships are not the most important focus despite all our conditioning, and it is important especially for women to remember this, as they often feel there is something lacking in their lives if they are not part of a couple. Nowadays both women and men deal with this by throwing themselves into work. A primary relationship is not essential, but if we are not in touch with people and don't have good relationships with our friends, then something is wrong. Relationships come about through the law of attraction, which is increased when you make social relationships a priority.

Have inner peace. What is inner peace? Many people are trying to find it, but it is not to be found anywhere. Inner peace is the movement of having no need for justification, no reaction to whatever is there. There is only direct observation of whatever is happening, without any identification. This means engaging in the art of not taking things on a personal level. Only then can you be in a process of inner peace.

Have no reaction. No reaction is always connected with inner peace. They go together hand in hand. No reaction does not mean that you do not have your standpoint, that you do not say no to things, that you do not create your own boundaries. No reaction means reacting only through the atmosphere of slow feelings. It is *wu wei*, or doing in not doing. It is a question of having balance.

Be humble. Sometimes a situation arises in which we come to realize how insignificant we are, which creates a sense of humility. We realize that we have no influence on how the wind blows, but, on the other hand, we recognize our tremendous potential. We realize that we can decide how to set the sails of the boat that is our being, our life. This creates the slow feelings of bliss and love. In all of this, the most difficult thing to learn is the art of not defending ourselves. It is a natural reaction and part of our survival instinct to reject whatever is new and to protect what is old and familiar. It might seem that we are playing safe, but this reaction can be destructive because it hinders growth. We protect ourselves by holding on, blocking, arguing, justifying, creating diversions and indulging in addictions. The process of not defending happens not only in relation to other people and their ideas; it is also about not defending within – in every cell, every muscle and the various images we have of ourselves. The attitude of not defending activates the soul or the energy body. The less defended we are, the more love there is. The mystics spoke of surrender, but this is not the same as no resistance. One can have resistance to certain beliefs, for example, and yet still be in a general atmosphere of not defending. It seems to make sense to defend ourselves, our homes, our country and our values, but all these forms are transitory and can only be protected for a limited period of time. The soul is the only thing worth protecting, yet paradoxically it is protected best by the act of not defending. Not defending, as an expression of love, is ultimately the only long-term strategy for survival.

The Soul
My Soul
Can be felt
by me ... thats my intuition
Speaking to me in the energy soul vibrating

CHAPTER 11

Creating the Atmosphere of the Qualities

To sum up so far, we have seen that psychological problems represent symptoms of repressed and overshadowed qualities. The essence of your being is the energy body or the soul, which, although we cannot observe it, can be felt as an atmosphere, and the qualities are a part of this essence that we can perceive directly. This essence gets overshadowed over time by our *second birth*, or the birth of thoughts, so that we are constantly concealing our strengths.

We saw how the future without perspective is fear, and fear is thought. We need to learn how to distinguish between the different thought processes, and this can only be done from the level of the qualities. There is a distinction between the motivative thought process, which is a communion, and the associative thought process, which is a constant description of what should be the communication. Through the associative process, or the ego, thinking becomes its own tool. We do not love, we think love and we do not act, we just think of action. In this way, the qualities become increasingly overshadowed. So we have to learn to observe thinking if we want to blend the qualities, the atmosphere of the qualities and thinking. The result of this blending would mean that the inner intelligence would leave behind time-space duality and the ego. We can see from this how the associative thought process hinders us from direct perception. It is the process of constant description that not only overshadows the qualities but also creates a resistance toward slow feelings.

Slow feelings and our qualities

Fast feelings stem from aggression and its different manifestations such as jealousy and greed, all of which are a symptom of fear, and fear itself also belongs to the fast feelings. Remember that when we experience fast feelings there is an input of energy because of a situation. For example, say you feel betrayed by a friend. You feel a surge of jealousy; there is a minute or two when you experience an input of adrenaline, and then it is gone. It then requires the associative thought process to keep the whole process alive. In a case like this the body's hormonal system, the flight-or-fight reflex, is over very quickly.

The associative process eventually renders us unable to distinguish between the act of actual doing and thinking about doing, and this creates a hindrance not only for our qualities but also for the manifestation of slow feelings, which is the vehicle in which the qualities are carried. The slow feelings such as love, joy, inner peace, ecstasy, happiness and compassion are feelings that cannot be affected by this kind of hormonal activity, which means that most of the time the qualities are thought about but not really lived.

You may have observed by now how tremendously difficult it is to really be in touch with our potential. When we try to be in touch with our qualities, the mind immediately jumps back into negativity and claims that staying with the atmosphere of the qualities is too difficult to do; you may feel that you still do not have sufficient contact with your qualities or that there are still too many blockages within you, for example. The reason the mind does this has very simply to do with the principle of evolution in that we do not need our qualities for survival. The first level of our awareness is the form or body. When we come into form, the essence of a baby is its qualities; however, the qualities are structured within the body, and the baby does not have an awareness of its quality. It is not aware of it because it *is* the quality. The baby is only aware of the body: is it cold or too warm, is it hungry or not, in a pleasant position or not? The first thing that the mind learns to do with awareness is to be alert to the problems of the body. It watches for any hint of unease in the body. If there is an uneasiness in the body, even if it is only hunger, it acts accordingly to relieve the unease.

In the process of growing up the mind learns to focus on the negative, simply because survival is based on being watchful for anything that may be wrong. The mind is trained to be constantly aware of something going wrong and becomes totally fixed on the idea that as long as there is nothing wrong within the body, and as long as there is no imminent danger, there is no need for action. It is not focused on what is good, and so it learns through the associative thought process to do exactly the same thing on the psychospiritual level.

The mind and safety

As we have seen, we can create a history and an explanation with a problem or a weakness, and whenever the mind sees the possibility of creating a cause, it creates the illusion of security. Security, as we know, eases the mind. It can even justify absurdities; for example, there are cases where the mind feels more at ease if it can be convinced that a person has cancer because of some past life issue. The mind is more comfortable with the most far-fetched explanation than it is with staying with whatever may be there at any given time. The mind is not even ready to entertain the possibility that whatever problem you have, the problem is still not as big as your quality.

Our qualities are there, however, despite you or any of our efforts. You cannot develop them or get rid of them; you cannot even take credit for them. You cannot go into lengthy explanations about the qualities when they have nothing to do with you personally. It is just part of the life force, our *qi*, and you were born with them. The essence therefore is far more vast than the problem.

Imagine that you are forty years old with two children, and you have been diagnosed with terminal cancer. In such a situation I cannot imagine anyone wishing to die. Imagine that you are spiritually "advanced" to the point where you do not object to the thought of death, but you still worry about what will happen to your two children of five and eight years of age after your death. Once you have actually died you will realize that despite all the psychological pain and sorrow for your children, and all the physical pain due to the cancer, your qualities have not been destroyed.

The trauma of coming into this world and manifesting in a material structure focuses us too much on the material level. You can look around you and see how our society is incredibly obsessed with the body. If people spent the millions that they put into health and care of their bodies on caring for their qualities, the world would be a better place. This is not, of course, to suggest that we should not take care of the body, but there has to be balance. The balance becomes possible when the mind can see that constantly watching out for that which might be a danger, for whatever you feel is not good in you, is a huge barrier to expression of the qualities. We can easily create a greater barrier by judging ourselves.

This is just how the mind functions; we need to just be aware of why it is happening. Our qualities want to be able to come into expression, to be used and to be lived. Once we are in touch with our qualities we realize how valueless it is to invest time and energy in looking at the past.

Perspective and association

The person who says that they have been harmed by their past and seriously believes that to be true will be viewing the past from a negative perspective. We cannot really see our past as it was, so what is the use of looking at it? If, however, you are healthy, intelligent and without problems, you will see the past as it truly was. If you are functioning out of a neurotic structure, you will see nothing other than what it is to look at something from a neurotic structure. This then becomes a psychological game.

If you go into therapy with a therapist who has not found inner peace, joy or happiness and has not embraced or been penetrated by the atmosphere of their respective qualities, then they will be deceiving themselves and also their clients. The clients are part of this deception, as they believe that someone else is better placed than themselves to tell them who they are. In situations like this the less the therapist is in touch with their own atmosphere, the less space they will give the client.

Giving a client space means that the therapist is not subscribing to psychoanalytical theories of resistance, repression, the unconscious or even spiritual theorizing such as whether or not people have achieved a certain level of enlightenment. Any readers of this book who are thinking of consulting a therapist are advised to bear this in mind and avoid a therapist who tries to fit a client into a frame by labelling, defining or interpreting within the confines of a theoretical structure.

There is a beautiful saying from a spiritual tribe in Africa: "The laws of nature cease to exist in the person who is penetrated by God." In other words, the more we are in touch with our qualities, then the less the need to adhere to whatever laws there may be. Laws or rules are a description of something we observe. What we fail to realize is that the description is only valuable at the very moment of observing and may not be applicable again.

The past in fact means the absence of the qualities because the past does not project into the present. If we go back to the beginning and consider how the future creates the past, try to penetrate this statement on a feeling level, not by understanding it intellectually. Qualities are blocked because of the past. Both Buddhism and Christianity give us hints and guidelines in the Four Noble Truths, the Eightfold Path and the Ten Commandments, and in the *Bhagavad Gita* Krishna says that enlightenment has nothing to do with reincarnation or the past.

If we limit our understanding to the associative thought process, it will hinder us from developing a perspective for the future. The qualities become blocked as a result of identifying with both the past and the future. Jesus said, "Be like the flowers in the field," meaning do not be concerned about the past, about that which has happened or is happening, as paradise – the future – lies somewhere else. If you are concerned with the past and give descriptions to it, the future loses its perspective and becomes fear.

Krishna was a revolutionary because in his time, the karma and reincarnation belief system was heavily subscribed to, and sadly it remains so now. He attacked it directly by saying that reincarnation is not there to be understood, to be turned into a description or for us to find out what has happened in past lives and to elucidate what has gone wrong. To do this would only encourage us to identify with the past and be a hindrance to our future. The creation of a perspective for our lives can be brought about only by expressing our qualities.

In order for us to penetrate the mind and our thinking processes, we need to understand the mind's source, its own root. To go back to the image of white light being broken down into different colors, white represents consciousness, and when consciousness is broken down into pieces, this simply means that we become aware of a particular thing and then we have thoughts centered around it. This means that the idea of unconscious and conscious is an absurd theoretical concept. It is very important to understand this simply because once we are in touch with the qualities, the mind can pretend that we cannot be directly in contact with them. You may feel a little confused about your qualities – maybe you think there are still some unconscious problems that you have not worked with or have repressed.

This is a beautiful way out for the mind. It creates a barrier through all of these excuses for why it may not be possible to be in touch with the qualities.

Conscious and unconscious mind

Part of the shadow is created by thought out of the duality that exists when energy is split. The thought process splits the mind into the conscious mind and the unconscious mind. Thought behaves as if there was a distinction between conscious mind, unconscious mind, consciousness and mind. Remember the white color is white until it is refracted into colors. If we take the white color as the unconscious mind, once it's broken into colors, it becomes the conscious mind. It is as if there were three levels separated from each other. What happens with thought is that in the end you firmly believe that what you are thinking is reality.

There is in fact no separation between the unconscious and conscious, or qualities and problems. If we believe that there is a separation, then we become locked in a fight between qualities and problems. There is only one mind from which consciousness is showing us only a part. If you look at a picture and change your focus from one part to another, you can never see the picture as a whole. You will see it differently at different times, even though the picture remains the same. What is conscious is constantly changing.

There is no boundary between unconscious and conscious; there are only levels where the conscious mind is less aware of things because the mind, through thought, creates barriers. These barriers come about through our belief systems, and this limits perspective. We are influenced not only by how we see but also by how we are aware. The quality of our perception depends on our awareness; for instance, when we are tired we will have a different awareness. If you are an architect at an art exhibition and there are some paintings with buildings in them, you will be drawn to them first. If, however, you are keen on pornography and go to the same exhibition, then the first pictures that will strike you are the ones with nude women.

This happens not because the other parts of your awareness are repressed or unconscious but because your thoughts have an influence over what you most want to see. It is not that the quality is unconscious and the problem is here in the conscious, nor that there is an unconscious problem and therefore the quality is not present – these are all just mind games.

What does it mean to see this as a process for the future, as a perspective for our lives? First, there is no unconscious and conscious. Indulging in the concept of the unconscious is like splitting time into the past and the future. The unconscious becomes the past; the conscious becomes that which will be possible in the future. Neither time nor consciousness can be split in this way, otherwise transformation cannot take place.

A transformation in consciousness – not in the unconscious or the conscious but in consciousness as such – can only happen when we bring an end to identification. Krishna said, "Only when you stop identifying with the past will you be free from what you were and what you will be." Only when we end our identification with the past will the soul ever become free from what we think we are but we are not, free from what we think we do but we do not, free from what we think it was and it will be. Only then does the soul have real freedom. Liberation comes by not identifying with the past, and this in turn creates the freedom from what was and what will be, from what you think you were and what you think you will be.

If we are honestly just observing without adding to or taking away anything that is there, we can never be totally sure of our qualities. This is because qualities cannot be learned and therefore cannot be identified with. They neither come from the past nor move into the future, therefore we cannot identify with them. We can never be 100 percent sure how long they will be manifest. We cannot know how they will manifest and whether they will manifest at all. One quality may manifest in childhood in a particular way and then suddenly manifest differently at another time. All we can do is to simply be in touch with them.

The music of the qualities

Imagine the qualities as an orchestra with a violinist, a pianist, a drummer, a cellist, a trumpeter. The instruments represent all the different qualities you possess. They are all playing the same piece of music. Your mind, however, is able to jump from one instrument to another. At one moment it is observing the cellist, then it jumps to the violinist. The cellist is still there, and from the violinist the mind may turn to the pianist, which does not mean that the woman playing the violin no longer exists. She is still playing, but the mind is focusing more on the woman who plays the piano. Sometimes we need to hear the piano, sometimes the violin. Then when we bring them together as an orchestra, we hear all the instruments playing the same tune at the same time. This is the atmosphere of the qualities.

When we listen to the music as a whole, we are not sure which instrument is more dominant, but it is the whole, the music as such, the atmosphere that matters most. When it comes to our qualities, we may not be able to distinguish them nor be clear about which quality is dominant. As we cannot identify with any one quality, and because it is difficult to listen to the atmosphere, we prefer to escape to the comfort of identifying with our problems.

Krishna was aware that the human mind was a psychological mind, constantly running back to its problems and then blaming itself or others for being stuck there. We have to learn to surf between the two worlds – not because one world is unconscious and one is conscious but because the mind cannot possibly see everything at the same time. The mind has to gently move from place to place, just as it does when we listen to an orchestra. It is important that we keep time out of all of this, that we do not start to calculate how long certain qualities manifest for and make deductions about which one is more important or necessary. The key is to keep the picture of the whole composition.

Surfing between the different levels of quality and thought, or between out-of-body consciousness and mind consciousness, can only happen through slow feelings. We simply cannot surf on fast feelings because there is no flow; unlike slow feelings, they create reactions on the body level that interfere with the possibility for direct observation. The only way to get to slow feelings is by establishing the connection to sadness. Sadness counteracts or neutralizes fast feelings. Sadness is the bridge between this world and the other world, between fast feelings and slow feelings of sadness, love, joy, compassion and inner peace. Sadness is the representation of qualities that are not lived, and the more we repress feelings in general, the more sadness there is.

The repression of either slow feelings or fast feelings makes it difficult for the qualities to manifest. The medium through which the qualities can be expressed is the slow feelings. If qualities are our essence, then whenever we repress slow feelings it is like taking the instrument away from the quality, and there is automatically sadness. Whenever we become aware of this repression, what comes up is sadness. Therefore, if nature is as it is, and we overshadow our qualities, then whenever we begin to get in touch with our qualities, we come to the first level of awareness, which is sadness and the bridge to the slow feelings. The state of being deeply touched by ecstasy or joy cannot and does not come before this part of sadness.

The Buddha experienced enlightenment only after he had seen misery, suffering and sadness. The word *suffering* is misused now and no longer refers to suffering in the true sense of the word. Suffering in our century means pain and bad luck, but in the Buddha's time it also meant sadness. If we try to avoid sadness we will never be enlightened; we will never be free. Jesus said, did you think I came to bring you love? Before love I bring the sword, which is sadness. Through the ages spiritual messengers have urged us not to avoid sadness. It will help to avoid fast feelings like self-pity, but do not avoid crossing over the bridge of sadness. We have all accumulated the tendency to concentrate only on that which is not good in each of us and forget what is good in us, to split our consciousness into unconscious and conscious.

We have accumulated this tendency simply because the birth of the essence is overshadowed by thought. The problems then show as rebellious qualities, and when we begin to wake up we find ourselves walking on the bridge of sadness. If we then stop and hold back the feeling, we block our qualities again and increase the sadness. The Buddha called this the karma of sorrow, and he meant only that if we stop feelings of sadness from manifesting, there is no purification and renewal. The purification or cleansing of our soul and of our system does not come through love, but through sadness. You cannot create sadness. If we try to create sadness, we create nothing other than a kind of seriousness, an ugliness, but not actual sadness. The moment we try to create sadness we encounter the "isms" like racism, sexism and spiritual fascism, but we do not get in touch with sadness. Sadness is only possible, says Krishna, with no identification.

Self-pity increases identification or personalization. If the process of identification is the root of our problems, then it will also be a problem if used in relation to the qualities. We need to take care not to identify with a quality, otherwise it will become tainted. If we feel some confusion, it will help us to focus on the atmosphere of the quality rather than the quality itself. Going back to our previous analogy, do not focus on the piano, the violin, the cello or the trumpet; focus only on the whole sound of the orchestra. This does not mean that all the instruments are of equal value all the time – that would be unnatural, and some will, according to the situation, take the leading role.

Again, consider the words of Krishna: if you identify with the past, there is no future, no perspective. If you identify with one color, you ignore the other colors. If you identify with one quality, then you risk not ever knowing the qualities that you may still not have discovered.

The characteristics of atmosphere

The mind will always want assurances of what the atmosphere is like and how to know when it is in the atmosphere of the qualities. There are a few indicators because the atmosphere has its own characteristics, independent of whatever quality is there.

If you are listening to an orchestra, the atmosphere of the music is the same whether the violin is more dominant or the percussion instruments are absent – it is the atmosphere as a whole that is important.

Awareness. The process of awareness grows out of our observation. It is the releasing of old patterns and the constant process of detachment.

Respect. The process of respect is the will to see things as they are – not adding or taking away anything from what is there. Respect means we have no desire to manipulate the qualities but just to see them as they are.

Acknowledgement. To acknowledge something means to say "yes" to an observation without wanting to change it. We acknowledge without judging. We admit to seeing the situation and are prepared to leave it at that. It is affirming whatever you see.

Gratitude. This is a word that the Buddha often used. The process of gratitude is simply to recognize life and its qualities and nothing more than that.

Humility. This is our only true protection against power games or egoism. We may hope for protection by other means involving ritual or belief, but usually the result is that we only increase our egoism. According to the law of attraction, so long as we have humility we cannot be hurt.

Simplicity. Simplicity is the process of not adding anything that does not belong to what is already there. In Christianity it means not to lie or not to betray. We tell thousands of stories using our minds, and although half of our storytelling does not have to do with lying, the other half is pure fantasy. We habitually add something to make ourselves look a little better, more interesting or a little worse than how we actually are. Simplicity is the process of not adding anything. It sounds simple, but it can be enormously difficult.

Trust. Trust means we do not to cling to time, and we try to be patient, which is really the process of not being concerned about time. Using only our mind we can never trust completely; the mind is structured in time, so we cannot trust through an effort of mind. Trust can only come through being present in the atmosphere of the qualities.

Surrender. This word is so misused: what comes to mind is surrender in war to the enemy, surrender to the person who is stronger, surrender to the government, surrender to spirit. Surrender is simply the process of forgetting ourselves; it is faith. To surrender is to be totally absorbed in something. In the same way that we cannot trust by using the mind, we cannot forget ourselves through the processes of the mind. We cannot instruct ourselves to forget ourselves. It happens only in the atmosphere of the qualities because the qualities have nothing to do with us personally.

Vulnerability. Vulnerability is the ability to be hurt. It is important to remember that this refers to vulnerability in the psychospiritual sense and not on the level of the body – the idea is not to invite physical harm but to be open to the possibility that some things will hurt us and not to defend ourselves against what might or might not happen. To be vulnerable psychologically and spiritually creates strength, as clearly shown in the martial arts. In trying to be strong we create weakness, but if we are simply open to whatever is there, we create strength. In the words of Lao Tzu, "A stone may look strong, but a constant drop of water on the stone will destroy it." If we look at vulnerability in terms of energy, a blockage can give the illusion of strength in the short term because it stops us from focusing our awareness on troublesome areas in our lives.

Eventually, however, if we do not integrate the parts of our lives or ourselves that we have shut out, we will be unable to avoid a collapse of some kind later on. To be a vibrational being free of blockages is to be a free-flowing system of energy that is vulnerable and open to the new and unknown and is alive and strong.

Love. Love is to be found within every atmosphere of the qualities and is simply the movement toward that which is new. The moment we stop being attracted to whatever is new, then we are no longer in the flow of love. In a relationship, if we stop seeing the person in front of us as someone who was a certain way yesterday but will probably be different today, then love fades away. The Buddha called it *detachment*, and Krishna called it *no identification*. Therefore, it is impossible for us to love ourselves as a personality. We have to see that the ego represents that which is old, and love is always the movement toward that which is new.

Each quality has this atmosphere then that is made up of these characteristics that we can sense and that create our actions: awareness, respect, acknowledgement, gratitude, humility, simplicity, trust, surrender, vulnerability and love. The person who walks within this atmosphere is not going anywhere – not into the future nor into the past. There is no stability either because there is constant change. In this atmosphere one becomes free so that the soul can fly.

CHAPTER 12

Moving Toward a State of Being

As we go through every stage of development or enlightenment, we also pass through a phase where there is a danger of our experience being lost again. If something happens quickly, then this risk of losing the experience is even greater – for example, there is always a risk of depression if an experience of overwhelming love cannot be completely integrated. As Evelyn Underhill put it: "It is the last painful break with the life of illusion, the tearing away of the self from the World of Becoming, in which all its natural affections and desires are rooted, to which its intellect and senses correspond, and the thrusting of it into that World of Being where at first, weak and blinded, it can but find a wilderness in the dark."

There can be no transmutation without fire. All the great spiritual teachers of our time agree in describing the three stages of stress, tribulation and loneliness as being an essential part of the way from the Many to the One, from suffering to love, from duality to oneness, from separation to interconnectedness.

Trust the tide
Imagine you are watching the sea, and you notice two things: one is the water as such and the other is the waves. The waves are born out of

the water and return to it as they die. Imagine that the water represents out-of-body consciousness, and the ripples or the waves represent mind consciousness or thoughts. The water represents the energy body, while the waves represent the mind structure.

Now picture in your mind a guitar and its strings. When you touch a string it creates a sound that is not created by the string itself but by the body on which the string is strung. The strings represent our thoughts, and the body of the guitar that creates the resonance represents consciousness. The guitar represents the energy body, and the strings represent the mind. Whenever the wave or the guitar string wants to become independent, or whenever the string thinks it is able to create sound without the body, then it will create tension. It will either be too loose because it tries to be separate and detaches from the body or it will be too tense and snap.

The wave represents the playing aspect of consciousness, which is the water. Can the wave be aware of the water, or, in other words, can thought be aware of consciousness? Is there real awareness when consciousness is aware of thought; is there a real awareness when the water is aware of the wave, when the body of the guitar is aware of the string or the other way around?

Is the drop of water falling into the ocean melting with the ocean or is the drop of water falling into the ocean making the ocean become the drop? From pure observation, we can see that when thought becomes aware of consciousness, things will most likely become more complicated. When consciousness becomes aware of thought, however, then bliss and enlightenment follow.

For example, say you are at a lecture, and the speaker at this lecture is talking about karma. You do not know how the lecturer derived his ideas about karma and you hear him saying sensitive words like love, reincarnation, God, hate, Buddha, souls and angels. The listening part of your consciousness, if it simply stays as consciousness, or water, is just observing and allowing the information to filter through. If, however, you are listening out of what we earlier described as the "wave" aspect, then you are no longer listening to receive information. Then a debate begins within your mind, and at the end of the talk you will go up to the lecturer and argue about how you have heard other masters speak differently on the subject of karma.

If, on the other hand, you are in a state of receptive consciousness, you might think, "Who cares about the other masters?" not out of a lack of respect for them but simply because there is no need to bring them into the situation. You would also focus on your own observations in regard to what was said. If you receive everything purely as information until you have made your own observations, you will not be so preoccupied with defending an ideology. What anyone says about anything is not as important as what you observe about it.

Even if someone you admired and respected told you exactly how karma works from observations out of their own perspective, it would not help you one little bit if you did not support this with your own observation.

Trust your observation
The first law of spirituality is to deeply respect everyone and their own particular teachings or information but to not rely on them even if they are a guru, a master or an authority because blind belief will not help in your transformation. Only your own observation can ever transform you. If your observation is different from the observation of a so-called guru, it will transform you more than his knowledge as knowledge in your head. Use as much information as you can, but be aware that if you make observations of processes based only on this information, then the process is worth only half as much as if you were to first observe the process for yourself and then get confirmation of the observation from some source of information.

Rely only on the direct observation you have made independent from any information. Spirituality is about learning to ask questions based not on theoretical, philosophical, methodical structures but on your own completely independent observation. You can philosophize for the rest of your life about love. One person says love means this, someone else says it means that. There are hundreds of different possible definitions for love. Love is simply the movement toward the new, and you will find thousands of possibilities to contradict that rationally. It is what you observe in yourself about love that matters. If your observation is that love is about staying with the old and familiar, this will be the action of love. It does not matter how you describe it; the action will create love.

Whenever thought is arguing with thought, it is dealing with the "finger pointing at the moon," not the moon itself. It is focusing on the string of the guitar instead of seeing that the string is only a medium for the body-mind consciousness and a means for creating the music. The wave is simply the playful aspect of consciousness.

Can you allow your mind to be so awake that it can stay focused on one's own observation, which is the only thing of value, even if it is totally contradictory to someone else's observation and information? The Buddha, Jesus, Mohammed and Krishna all acted out of their respective observations even though they were in direct contradiction to what anyone else may have been saying at the time.

Observation is always revolutionary. To adapt your thought to something that is already established can be gratifying, but it has nothing to do with transformation. When we considered the meaning of surrender, we saw that the connection with the atmosphere does not mean surrendering to a person, a master or a guru. No mystic has ever said surrender to me. Surrender means to base your ideas only on what you can see, feel and think in your observation about yourself. It means not making a single compromise because of what other people are saying. Truthfulness, which is a beautiful quality, does not mean to stand up and fight because you believe you are in the right and everyone else is wrong. It means to relax in one's own observation and not to deny it even if everybody says it cannot possibly be like that.

The scientists are today's mystics. Good scientists will always base their ideas on their own observation first and then offer it to others. If others do not arrive at the same observations, the scientist does not just stop and give up. The art of transformation takes courage, which is another quality of observation, and authenticity, which means to stay with that observation even if it looks totally wrong. If Jesus had stopped trusting his own observation simply because his teachings were different from those of his contemporaries, would Christianity have come into existence? If the Buddha, who was constantly attacked by scholars, philosophers and religious people in his time, had given up because he was made a fool of when they attacked him, saying that his observations were nonsense, where would Buddhism be?

Trust your own observations not because yours are better or closer to the truth than anyone else's but because your own path and your own transformation only happens when you follow your own observations. When the guitar string is touched, or when we have a thought, a vibration is created so that the sound can be heard. The sound is similar to our observation and is a part of consciousness, not thought. To be spiritual therefore means to depend only on ourselves for our transformation, to be rebellious, to be revolutionary.

Direct communication

I once asked Krishnamurti what the biggest problem was in communicating directly with an audience, and he replied, "When I am communicating with people, they always immediately go to their reservoir of knowledge, which most of the time is not even theirs. They go to their knowledge instead of communicating with me from their direct observation." When I asked him what then happens as a result of this, he replied, "Look, it is very simple, there is no real communication."

Can you imagine what would happen if someone says to you "I love you," and you say, "I don't understand, can you describe what you mean, how do you love me?" R. D. Laing, one of the great psychiatrists, said that we can never experience what another is experiencing, but we can enter into a communion with them through our own experience. We cannot understand what a person means when they say, "I love you" – we can only observe whether or not we feel something that we call love for this person.

Going back to the two analogies of the sea and the guitar, perhaps we can understand more easily what is meant by *atmosphere*. The quality, or atmosphere, and the knowledge of this quality is the strength. It has to be touched to create sound. The quality is the wave, but the quality independent of consciousness, which is the water or the string on the guitar, does not create anything. The string, independent of the guitar, can try to vibrate on its own for as long it wants, but it will not produce a sound. When slow feelings meet the quality, an atmosphere is created.

The atmosphere is a movement of slow feelings and the qualities coming together in a communion, a marriage, a state of being. The atmosphere is a state of being, and in that communion, consciousness is aware of thought, and then there is not the feeling of love but the state of love, not the feeling of a quality but the state of quality.

Feeling and being

There is a difference between *feeling* and *being*. A state of being does not have a consciousness separate from consciousness. It is not aware of love or quality; it is simply consciousness. When the slow feelings of love, joy, bliss, happiness, sadness and compassion melt with quality, you arrive at what is called a state of being. A state of being does not mean that you feel feelings; you just are. So you would not feel love, but be love. When something is love or is a quality, it is a state of being and not a feeling, so there is no consciousness of it. Once there is the feeling of love, there is the separation of being conscious of feeling love, as opposed to the state of consciousness called love. You just fall into a state of consciousness. One of the simplest of Jesus's teachings is that in order to enter what we call heaven, we have to be as innocent as children, which means we are not aware and not separated from awareness. We are neither the doer nor the doing, the awareness of loving nor love.

In Greek mythology the word *demon* originally meant the devil. However, by adding good to evil we get *evdaemonia* as Plato called it – the happiness of the soul. The demon or the weakness then becomes the quality; there is no separation between good and bad. Separation happens when the wave wants to be more aware of itself than of consciousness or when the string wants to create the music. In human terms, we then become unhappy. When we are in the state of being, or in consciousness, the wave is just a manifestation of consciousness, and it becomes the evdaemonia.

In this state of evdaemonia, the *daemonia* or weaknesses, are what Plato called the *metaxy* or the go-between for the soul. How we deal with our problems is our way of getting in touch with the soul, and in this we can see that any adversity in our lives must be used as our guide and not a demon to be exorcised.

Developing insight

We can understand the depth of what Krishna meant when he told Arjuna to go to war. Arjuna was horrified by this, as he felt war was something to be abhorred. War is the symbol for all that we see as evil, and it is also a metaxy – a go-between. There is nothing in this world that does not involve a movement toward the soul. If we pick up a guitar and just touch a string, even if we do not know how to play the melody, the sound will transport us to consciousness. Even if it sounds terrible, it still gives us a sense of the soul.

No matter how complicated or difficult a problem may be, the qualities are constantly influencing, forming our being and our life. The go-between cannot be killed. The wave can do whatever it wants; it can never be separated from the water. It also does not matter how we live in this world. If we are good or bad, this will not have an influence on the soul. Neither the soul nor the qualities can be altered by our actions. Whatever we do is part of consciousness and will only create more consciousness.

The influence of the quality, on the one hand, and you, on the other, in evolving toward the quality – whichever way you deal with it, whichever route you take – creates another blending, another contribution. This is how life or living is created. This is why some religions say that the problem is not about what you do or whether you do good or bad; the problem has more to do with whether or not you can see what you have done wrong and if you can forgive yourself for it. Can you develop an insight into how you deal with things? If a person always does wrong, it means they have not reached a level of consciousness that can understand the mistake. Mistakes as such are the result of actions born out of a lack of awareness. Whenever we act without being first aware of our thoughts, we run the risk of our actions looking like mistakes when we see them in hindsight.

We all make mistakes, but not because we are inherently bad. Imagine what happens when the wave focuses too much on consciousness instead of consciousness focusing on the wave. We become dominated by thought and feeling, we have lost touch with the state of being and the communion or *samadhi* cannot happen. The state of being is *nirvana*. The communion is the movement toward nirvana and is known as samadhi or enlightenment, or to use the Christian mystical term *the receiving of the Holy Spirit*.

Heraclitus said, "A man cannot change his character." Character is the symbol for everything that is our essence. This is much more than what we can accumulate through our history. It refers to the qualities, or the soul. The wave cannot affect consciousness, as consciousness does not change. The water as a whole remains as the ocean, and the wave's efforts to be aware of the water will only lead to distress. It is consciousness that has to be aware of thought; the essence, which is unchanging, has to be aware of body-mind. Body-mind trying to become aware of consciousness is an impossibility – this is like the tail trying to wag the dog or the cart pulling the horse. The wave is thought; thought is the accumulation of knowledge; knowledge is the past, and the past is the ego, the I. Communion will only happen when the ego or the I can see its function – when the waves see that they are there as the playful aspect of consciousness or when the guitar string can see that it represents the physical aspect of the sound. This can only happen when the ego realizes that it is simply a street sign showing us where to go; it is not the actual place.

As we saw earlier, the ego or I identifies with the body or form. It thinks it has similar boundaries and can defend itself just as the body defends itself, but the ego is made up of time, whereas the body is of form. We can defend our form, but we cannot defend time. In order to be in communion, the first thing the ego has to do is to shift from form to time. Only then can it move beyond space-time to non-duality or enlightenment. If the wave identifies with its form and then tries to hold on to it without merging into the whole, it will get into trouble; in doing this the wave simply cannot be joyful; it cannot interact with the other waves and becomes isolated.

Beyond space and time
Charisma is the gift of beauty and can be described as the absence of isolation. In practical terms we have charisma, or are charismatic in the eyes of others, when we are connected with the quality aura. Isolation is the absence of beauty. The wave needs to see that it is not form but is structured in time. It is born, and it will die. It is built out of the playfulness of the ocean; it is a part of consciousness, and it will go back to consciousness. All of this is possible only because it is of time, and therefore for a while it looks as if it was completely separate from

consciousness. Once it recognizes this it can relax and in so doing move to nonduality beyond space and time.

Listening to a piece of music without analyzing it, we assume a state of being. This is when thought structure three takes over, and the fore-future is constantly present. We are in the motivative thought process, which belongs to the movement toward nonduality and enlightenment. In a state of being, consciousness is not separated from the energy body, and it is in this state of metaxy that the quality gets activated. We are love without being conscious of love. We are no longer separated from consciousness and therefore not able to feel love, we are love and there is no separation.

Our deepest fear is seeing that we are powerful beyond measure. We are inseparable, free, pure consciousness with no limitation and no control. It is our light, not our darkness, that frightens us most. It is our soul and the qualities, not our problems, that terrify us. This state of being, which signifies the ending of the separation between consciousness and that which is conscious of consciousness, is the art of dying.

This does not mean that the waves are gone or that the strings are no longer present, but they do not want to be limited to their own life. Instead, they surrender to what they really are. The Buddha called it buddhahood or buddha nature. He said, "I am simply awake." A disciple asked a Zen master if a dog was buddha. A dog cannot talk about consciousness – it cannot reflect on questions of life, death and rebirth, but if we accept that a dog has the same source of consciousness, then it is buddha. When we eat a cow or a lamb we also take in the atmosphere of its consciousness, its buddhahood.

The end of separation

Can the mind cultivate a constant readiness to die? Dying does not mean that your sense of self is gone nor does it mean that you become a vegetable. Dying is a simple shift in focus when you realize that whatever you think, feel or act is merely a ripple of your consciousness as such. It simply means that whoever you meet, whatever your likes and dislikes may be, whatever you enjoy or detest in another person, these are all playful ripples of consciousness. Dying does not mean that we stop having our own opinions, but it does mean that we know that these are simply ripples that add to the consciousness of the world. Dying is not the absence of the I, it is when we realize that the I is an instrument for expressing the essence of the soul.

All religious teachings emphasize the need to serve. Serving has two aspects – one is to serve others, and the other, deeper meaning is the recognition that your whole being is in the service of the soul. How do we live our lives in serving consciousness, in the service of the soul? From this perspective, dying is not the end of the I – it is the beginning of a communion or marriage. Dying is the end of separation; it is the demon coming back to its source of evdaemonia.

In humans, then, the demon – weakness or the rebellious quality – works as the bridge between our body-mind and the soul. We become bridges between the planet, the world of nature and God, the Creator, the Tao or whatever you may wish to call it. When we are in stillness we have a glimpse of this oneness. Only then can the body-mind become the carrier of energy and love.

CHAPTER 13

The Art of Dying or Stepping Out of Time

If we want to learn how to die in life, we need to practice the process of getting in touch with what we have come to understand as the timeless observer. As we have seen, awareness can only come into being when there is no description involved. The moment we are aware of something, it is already a part of the past, and if we begin to describe what is happening, the flow of energy becomes blocked. There are six themes that we can use as guidance in observing this process within ourselves.

- Mind consciousness moves at a slower pace than the energy body or out-of-body consciousness, so do not block the flow through focusing on whatever is happening. Consciousness is awareness plus description. Whenever something comes into your awareness, do not describe it, but just be aware of whatever it is; allow it to become a transformative force.

- Remember that aggression is always a symptom of fear, fear is a symptom of sadness, and sadness or stillness forms a bridge to love.

- If aggression is a symptom of fear and fear a symptom of sadness, we need have no description and no interpretation. Awareness is possible without description. Only then can direct observation occur, and from this point, things become much easier.

- When we find the mind coming in to try to describe the root of thought, this just creates another thought. Try to focus only on the process, not the content. We can reach the root of thought only by ending all description. This is what meditation is all about. Realize that we never have just one thought. Everything is present, but not all is manifest, meaning that there are perhaps several thoughts in the background of our mind, yet only one is dominant.

Thoughts are there to support our biological system and to allow us to reflect, but the process of thought comes first, not the reflection. What we need to do is to just observe a process without interfering with it and then later reflect upon it, but most of the time we do just the opposite. We think first and then hope for a process as a result of our thinking. The idea that change can happen only after we have sufficient knowledge, or after we have completely understood something, is mistaken. The process happens in the reverse – change occurs first and understanding follows.

- The absence of thought creates a state of being in which slow feelings and atmosphere can be present. Once the description stops, we can sense something similar to feelings but more specifically slow feelings, which arise from a center of stillness. Whereas aggression arises from thought, sadness is born out of non-doing and the absence of thinking or movement. Every thought produces a feeling. All feelings are connected to thoughts; the root of feeling is thought. Every feeling can create a thought and therefore a movement of time. The absence of thought creates the absence of time. Absence of time is a moment of stillness; out of stillness comes the movement of love, and love is a movement toward the new. Hakuin, one of the greatest Zen masters, said, "At the moment when you no longer know what to think or even feel there is suddenly something more than thinking and feeling – there is enlightenment."

- We have a brain or mind consciousness and an out-of-body consciousness. We use our brain consciousness to deal with the movement of thoughts and feelings, and the out-of-body consciousness is made up of our atmosphere, which is part of our qualities. The anchor of the brain consciousness is structured within the body, in the brain. The out-of-body consciousness is anchored by the spiritual center, which lies over the heart and throat area.

Enlightenment is a metaphor for the act of being in touch with the atmosphere, or the out-of-body consciousness and the qualities. Enlightenment is the absence of energy described. It is an atmosphere beyond love, compassion and bliss. As you read these words, try to feel rather than think about the meaning.

These themes will help to bring us into contact with the *timeless observer*. When we observe our thoughts, we become a witness, a mind observer, which is part of our brain consciousness; the timeless observer is structured in the out-of-body consciousness, which involves a range of perception that lies beyond that of the brain. This is how we create the possibility of direct observation. Love or slow feelings are always connected with the timeless observer.

Out-of-body consciousness

Our brain consciousness involves the body, the mind and the aura system, which includes the etheric plus the mental aura. All religions and spiritual traditions point to the existence of something more than the consciousness of the brain. This something is the out-of-body consciousness, which includes the quality aura, the potential, the qualities and something else that can be called the soul or the other dimension.

We can observe the quality aura and the qualities, but we cannot really observe the soul. The part that we can observe is the energy body, and when we die, there is a clear separation between the brain consciousness and the out-of-body consciousness. For as long as we are alive, they are deeply interconnected or interrelated.

Brain consciousness, as we have seen, has to do with survival. The body-mind does not need music, love or joy – it only needs the means to survive. It is only on the psychospiritual level, or the movement from biopsychological consciousness to spiritual consciousness, that we respond to these things. To understand this we have to see that brain consciousness is a slower vibrational energy than the out-of-body consciousness. Whatever our experience, the moment we register it, at least 0.5 seconds have lapsed between the actual experience and awareness of it, so when we feel our energy moving and we try to describe it rather than just being with it, the flow is broken and we have created duality.

Weaknesses are born out of qualities in the sense that they come into existence because our ability to express our qualities has been disturbed in some way. Qualities are always a movement toward something new and unexplored, toward the fore-future. This is a movement that we cannot grasp with the mind. The mind is the past.

The I is the past; it is of time. We are constantly tempted to move to what can be seen in the past, and our interpretation of weaknesses is a part of the past. In this way, we keep returning to maya, or illusion.

What is really happening?

The process of being in touch with the timeless observer is the process of dying to the past and waking up to what is really happening, to the true nature of reality. The only thing that is certain in life is our death, and if we learn how to die while we are alive, we will be doing two things: we will facilitate the process (not the means) of our actual physical death, and we will free the qualities during our lifetime. To do this we have to learn how to disidentify with our body, to detach from thought and feeling, so that we can contact the energy body, the quality aura and the soul. Remember, it is not important to be able to define or describe but just to observe the quality aura.

Giving too much importance to the body or to feelings and thoughts limits the qualities, so we need to detach but take care not to reduce the validity of the body-mind – we are not aiming to become hermits or ascetics, and we are not pretending that our body-mind does not exist. We are trying to free ourselves from the fear of dying and, more importantly, from the fear of living. It is, after all, our constant fear of being in this life that is so destructive. The problem is not the ego itself but taking the ego as the center of our being and behaving as if the body-mind is the life essence. It is a bit like living in a house and then mistaking the house for all that we are. In fact, if we do not attempt to understand the process of dying, we cannot hope to live our lives fully.

Dying does not create conflict. Dying is the process of having absolutely no alternatives, and in this moment of realization, stillness arises. It is possible to achieve this stillness in our lives without having to physically die, by engaging in a dying process that involves a form of out-of-body consciousness. Death and dying is related to patience; when we have patience, we cease to care about time, and we live totally in the here and now, the fore-future.

We need to find a way to live every second of our lives as if it were our last, so we don't waste energy in pointless activity or postpone using our energy because we can never be sure if we will be alive later in the day. On the one hand, we never really know when we are going to die, and yet we put off really living as if we are certain that we will be here indefinitely. Next year, we say, we will sort out our lives. Until then, we fail to use our energy in living.

From the perspective of dying while living, there is no need to compete, fight, justify, achieve or struggle because it simply wastes energy. This is not a moralistic point of view. The point is that stepping out of time and duality and stepping into oneness automatically leads to being nonviolent, for example, as opposed to just believing in nonviolence. Once we have stepped out of time, there is love, and we all want love; we all want to be able to love.

A new experience

Why is it so difficult to step out of time, to get in touch with the dying process? What is there between death and birth? What is the similarity between death and birth? Another process similar to the process of birth and death is that of relationships. Death, birth and relationship share a common structure. When we are born, when we die and when we enter into a relationship it is always totally new. At the time of birth we cannot rely on past experience or on knowledge to assist us in coming into the world; we have only our temperament and our body, both of which are part of our heritage. We cannot rehearse death, just as we cannot rehearse life, so it is useless to rely on our experience. Even if we have had the most profound experiences that equip us with all the knowledge in the world, we cannot rely on it.

Birth, death and relationships are all totally new experiences, a journey into the unknown. For most people relationships are a tremendous adventure because we cannot plan them, and if we try to force the relationship, it will fall apart. Similarly, we cannot force the process of birth and death. In cases of suicide, where it appears as if death is being forced, we are active only in the phase of initiating it. Once initiated, the process of death is the same and is beyond control. Not a single soul that commits suicide is punished or stays in purgatory, any more than anyone who dies naturally. The process of dying is independent from the cause of death whether it is from a car accident, illness, a heart attack, old age or by committing suicide.

Whatever is new creates the sense of fear, which is the signal that we are moving toward something new, moving in the right direction. Fear is not the enemy. Imagine that you are coming toward something new and that this is the only way to take the next step in evolution, and you are constantly fighting it. If we can truly see how the process of fear happens whenever there is an input of something totally new and independent of our history, we become religious in the truest sense of the word, which has nothing to do with organized religion.

Anything new is bound to create fear because fear is the natural movement of evolution trying to maintain the status quo, while whatever is new is always threatening to replace the old and must elicit fear. Our body-mind can only be rearranged if we are ready to acknowledge the fear. Then, as the Buddha would have put it, the identification with the body-mind becomes more loosely connected. The attachment is weaker, and it is at exactly this moment that we feel a sense of fading away from the identification with the body-mind. Our consciousness then starts to expand.

Before enlightenment or dying, which is the total absence of the mind, we are not sure of where we are going because fear masks everything. We cannot avoid fear, and it is important that we do not fight it. Once we experience the expansion of consciousness, the process of dying starts all over again. Whenever our consciousness expands, we start to see and feel more, and old structures, belief systems and attitudes begin to fall apart. The opening of consciousness always concomitantly means the death of whatever has created an identification for itself. The ego, the I or the body-mind are simply restructured. Restructuring is the process of dying. In every death, therefore, there is a birth, and we open up to the unknown, to new things in our lives. The dying process depends on the birth of something new. Death does not happen without a concomitant process of birth.

Feeling love

In terms of energy then, what is the common ground between the dynamics of birth, death and relationships? The first thing that we see around a baby at the time of birth is the quality aura. The mental aura takes a further twenty-eight years to fully develop. The last thing we see after someone dies is also the quality aura. Imagine that you are asking yourself how you know when someone loves you. What conditions need to be present before you can say that someone loves you?

In order to believe that somebody loves you, you need to be able to really feel it, not just listen to someone saying "I love you." How do you know that these are their true feelings? If I tell you that a lemon has a sour taste, and you have never tasted a lemon, you simply will not know what I mean. The moment you taste a lemon you will know what I mean. You will be able to taste the lemon and its sourness because there are receptors on your tongue that are unique and independent from your history. If you were to remove these receptors, then you would not know what the sour taste of a lemon is like even if I tried to explain it to you in words.

In order to know that someone loves you, you need to have the ability to feel love within yourself. Even as a child you have the innate wisdom of love and can feel whether or not your mother loves you. This wisdom arises from the quality aura, so you already have love within you at the beginning of your life, which enables you to know immediately whether or not someone loves you. We are in fact nothing other than the flame of love. You are born with the ability to be love, to feel love, just as you were born with receptors on your tongue to taste different flavors.

When someone loves you, you recognize it immediately by their actions. You will never have the fear of not being loved. You may feel sad about not being loved, and the sadness of not being loved is in fact sadness that the person who does not love you denies you the ability to express your love toward them. The purpose of this body-mind is simply to carry the quality of love.

The quality aura is not an object located subtly somewhere in our magnetic field; it is the atmosphere that we generate around us. Each person has a specific atmosphere, which on the level of body consciousness relates to our temperament or character. If a child's temperament is to be shy, and his parents instill in him the idea that shyness is something negative, this is destructive of the child's qualities. Between the body-mind and the energy body, which is an atmosphere, there is space. Within this space the potential for everything manifests. Whenever we create a relationship between the qualities and the body-mind, we immediately create energy. Space creates energy. If we are too near to a person, or too far away, there can be no relationship.

In order to express ourselves, we all need a certain amount of space. Creating space is the movement of relationship in expression. Dying can happen only when there is space to move toward something new. Birth can happen only if there is space for that which is about to be born but which is yet unknown. If a baby about to be born could express what it was feeling, it would say, "I just went through a dying process." From our perspective as observers of the birth, we would say that we just observed a birth process. Someone who is dying would be aware only of being in the process of dying. The entity observing all of this from the other side would see a birth. Both processes need space, just as trees that are planted close together need to be able to grow. This space is the atmosphere.

Space and observation

We are all familiar with the feeling that we need space in relationship, but often we don't appreciate just how important it is to bring space into our emotions. We need to learn how to just observe our emotions or fast feelings, which are always connected with thoughts, in order to create space. We need to cease our identification with the body-mind to create enough space for the qualities to manifest. Then we will create the opportunity for the ongoing process of birth-death to happen freely instead of waiting until it is forced upon us at the end of our lives.

The atmosphere of the quality aura, or the energy body, is the birth-death process, the constant changing of things. We can now understand why Jesus said that we are only visitors in this world but not of this world. The I is time; the body is form. As a visitor, we need to try to be as gentle and unobtrusive as possible. In the process of dying and birth, the Hindu terms *sat*, *cit* and *ananda* – *satchitananda*, or "the cave of the heart" in which the new might be born – help us to clarify all of this. *Sat* means the endless, which means no time; however, the endless is only reached by the allowing of endings. *Cit* means the wisdom that can only be reached through changing. Wisdom is the constant renewal of knowledge. And *ananda* means bliss, which can only be reached through observing. *Ananda* is not a fixed state – it is present when we are in a state of just observing.

Observation is the key to the processes of birth and death. Whenever we express something to do with the process of dying, we also express birth. Birth and death cannot be separated, and to understand this process we need to look at it from the perspective of the observer. The *Bhagavad Gita* refers to the transcendental owner, the *paramatman*, as the atmosphere of the qualities.

The question is asked, "What is the difference between a living body and a dead body?" and the answer given is that the body is living only when the soul is integrated into it. A body is dead when the soul is not in the body and when the observer is present but is no longer using the body. From the perspective of the observer we see everything, including our fear and all our humanness, but we do not react to it. Reactions always involve using the mind, whereas observation means that we are in touch with the flow, the quality or atmosphere. Observation is independent from the mind. All the Zen masters insisted that as one cannot get rid of weaknesses, just watching the weakness with no reaction or description will make you the master of that weakness.

That transcendental owner or timeless observer is always there. We do not know what happens to it afterward, as we cannot observe it after death, but we can observe what is present here and now. We can observe the space and the atmosphere now. This is your Buddha nature, the Buddha in you or your Christ consciousness. It really does not matter what name you give it.

Can you start to see or feel that independent from your body-mind there is an atmosphere that is constantly present and that wants to be lived and fulfilled? To do this we have to shift from the observer that is constantly observing the body-mind to the observer that is observing, the timeless observer. We move from observing the unconscious body-mind to that which the body-mind is carrying around with it – the atmosphere of the energy body, the quality aura, the transcendental owner.

Wholeness

Why is it so important to experience this process of dying before the end of one's life, which may be thirty years or just five minutes away? At any moment, time could end, and you could be physiologically dead. If during the course of your life you are able to allow this space to exist without any identification, you create a tremendous amount of energy for life.

Healing of the body, mind and relationships – which is what life is built upon – and all the different forms of love rely totally on this process. It is always an individual movement, while at the same time a process that is similar for everybody. The sense of wholeness and oneness or unity emerge at the same time, just as in a relationship where *I* and *we* occur together. This is tremendously important because the nourishment we need for growth and healing of relationships and love all come out of this process of birth and death, which can be named broadly as religiousness.

The first thing we realize when we are in the process of religiousness is that there is absolutely no separation between the body-mind and the energy body. This is often described as "we are all one" – our interconnectedness. What does this really mean? If everything is everything else, if there is no separation, it means that every second you identify with your anger, or each time you justify it, you create an illusionary separation.

Each time we compare ourselves with someone else and feel frustrated because we think someone else is, for example, better qualified or more intelligent, we create an illusionary separation. This is like the illusionary separation between death and birth. We create isolation through such attitudes as comparison, antagonism, frustration, self-pity. Fundamentally, this means that our anger, jealousy and fear arise mainly because we are all human, not just because of our personal history.

Just as I would not be able to feel whether or not you love me if I did not already have the built-in structure of love, I cannot feel what you mean when you say that you hate me if I do not already have the built-in structure of hate. Aggression, fear, sadness, love, bliss are all about being human. The history or the content that we construct around it is what creates this illusionary separation.

Religiousness
In the process of religiousness we are able to recognize that our human body is just one out of many possible ways that form manifests in the universe. Identifying too much with the body is not only a problem for our body as such. In a broader sense, it creates nationalism, racism and cruelty toward animals that do not have the same body form and eventually can lead to fanaticism and destructiveness toward everyone and everything different from ourselves.

We also realize that each experience is unique but limited. For example, imagine that someone says they had an enlightening experience in which Jesus appeared. As a result of this experience this person believes he is right, and so the rest of the world has to follow his teachings. He is failing to appreciate that the uniqueness of one person's being also includes its personal limitations.

In a relationship, your experience of what your partner may have done may not be how your partner sees it – both of you are right because personal experience is unique but at the same time always limited to you. Where there is a birth, there is also a death. Where there is uniqueness, there is also limitation. Each time we bring out the atmosphere of our quality, we contribute to the atmosphere and quality of everybody else. In Buddhist terms, people known as Bodhisattvas, or enlightened beings, do not step out of the cycle of birth and rebirth but continue coming back into human form to help others become free, to carry on making a contribution to relieve the suffering of the world.

The limits of truth

It is important to realize that there is no truth. Whatever we feel, think or hear is only part of what is possible. It is never the whole truth, so admiring someone else's wisdom or being against new ideas, creating inner or outer authority figures, is useless. There is absolutely no authority. The most destructive authority is one's own mind and its identifications. We want so much to believe in the existence of an absolute truth so that we can then stop the process of dying. If absolute truth doesn't exist, then we have to live in the moment, ready to give up everything in the next moment, simply because everything we hear is only part of the truth. If we accept that there is no such thing as the truth, there is a continuous movement of dying then. We have to be totally vital. We cannot fall asleep because we have to live with the insecurity, which is love.

There is no entity judging us from above. The only person judging you is yourself. If someone says that they do not like you, they are judging themselves by projecting onto you what they do not like about themselves; they are expressing their attitudes, beliefs and perceptions. If you then feel hurt by this, it means that you are beginning to judge and limit yourself. In any given situation if something is said that you do not like, if you can see this and not personalize it or react to it, there is space between what was said and you, and you then are able to feel for the other, to understand their standpoint and create the energy of compassion and clarity.

Jesus said, if a seed does not fall on nourishing ground – or the atmosphere of the qualities – and does not want to die there, it will be alone. If it dies, it brings new life. The art of living is like the seed falling on nourishing ground. It is about being in the atmosphere of the qualities and letting the process of birth and death happen by itself. This allows for a constant new beginning. Everything we think of as weaknesses are defense mechanisms or labels for expressions of aggression. When we are in touch with the atmosphere of our qualities we stop judging; we drop our attitudes and our reactions. Then we are in emptiness, or stillness. Stillness is not the absence of noise; it is the absence of fear.

Chapter 14

From Sadness to Stillness

It is impossible to be in stillness if we are reacting to our feelings of fear. We can do this by escaping, by interpreting the past or by projecting into the future. If we escape into the future we often bring our aggression with us, while escaping into the past means we will probably be clinging to something or blaming someone. Once we stop being aggressive, we get in touch with fear. Fear is the signal that – although reflexively it makes us think something is wrong – indicates that we are getting in touch with something new and unknown. In order to deal with fear, it helps us to remember the three keys of responsibility, understanding and trust. With trust, we don't run away from the unknown, which always creates a moment of fear.

Wholeness and sadness
Sadness is not grief, nor is it self-pity. Self-pity is sadness identified with a cause and effect, which leads us into isolation. When we feel self-pity, the heart feels heavy. When we drop out of the I and realize that we are a part of the whole, we feel sadness. If we stay with the fear and realize that we are a part of the whole, our history becomes less important, and we move from the fear, which is a symptom of sadness, to sadness itself.

In portrayals of Jesus he always looks sad, and Krishna also taught that we cannot care for someone if we do not feel sadness. The Greeks made the distinction between Eros and Agape, or in the terminology of the Christian mystics, love and compassion. Love is always oriented toward something. As beautiful as it may be, love is connected with a desire. How long do we continue to love if we do not get anything back? The impersonal structure of sadness, on the other hand, brings us to caring or compassion. The movement of love and sorrow together results in compassion, and suddenly we are no longer fighting our body or struggling against our weakness. We feel sad about creating a history, or our individuality, and for isolating ourselves as a result of this, and it is exactly at this point that we open up to the qualities. We move to compassion, which is love that is not objectoriented. Sadness always increases energy when it is not personalized. It will always bring us back in touch with the atmosphere of stillness.

Healing and stillness

When we go into a church, a mosque or a holy place or when we are deeply in love with someone, we no longer talk about being in love; we talk about being touched. In both these situations we are taken over by feelings, and the personality just dissolves. When a baby is born, we do not talk about how much love we feel for it but instead find ourselves totally absorbed in being touched. This is really how healing comes about. Healing is the art of touching and being touched.

Loving a partner does not create stillness – it creates the urge for being together, for sharing, for sex, for enjoying life, all of which is beautiful. The level of being touched is born out of stillness. In this stillness there is an absence of any personal structure, and there can be sadness. We find ourselves in the absence of a personal structure, and at exactly the moment when there is this movement of sadness, if we can stay with it, we will discover that it does not return to being a symptom of fear and from there to a symptom of aggression. This creates all the freedom we need, and within that freedom is the energy of the life force.

This life force is a combination of wisdom and compassion, and we all have access to this the moment we stop focusing on our history. The way to be in touch with wisdom and compassion is to free ourselves from the images of the I or the ego and to not react with aggression, which is a symptom of sadness and fear. If we can stop reacting to our past and creating more of a history for ourselves, then we are bound to be in bliss, in inner freedom. The I transcends in not having to react, in not analyzing itself. It only transcends if it no longer has the need to react. Spirituality is the realization that transformation or transcendence only happens when there is no longer any need to react.

Cause and reaction

A problem may be looked into and understood, but it cannot be transformed by attaching labels or descriptions to it. It cannot be transformed through the illusion that our history relates only to ourselves or that our feelings of aggression, anger or fear are a purely personal experience. Feelings are often triggered by situations that allow us to see that there is a difference between a direct cause and a reaction to something or someone.

Psychologically there is no such thing as a cause. When, for example, a car breaks down, there is usually a cause – it has run out of fuel or something is wrong with the engine. The reason the car broke down is the result of a very simple mechanical problem, and this is the cause of it. In the human mind things are more complex, and our reactions are constructed from several factors, such as our tendencies, perceptions of ourselves and others and our conditioned behavior in relationship. For example, if you say, "I am always afraid of not being loved enough because my mother did not love me sufficiently," this does not explain why there are people from a similar background who are not at all afraid of not getting enough love.

In psychology a cause-and-effect theory is untenable. A mother who does not love her child may aggravate a preexisting serotonin problem in the child, which may give rise to feelings of not being loved enough.

On the other hand, a child may become more self-reliant in such circumstances, and then years later something might happen at school that acts as the trigger for a feeling of lack of love. There are usually at least three or four possible causes in every situation. For example, say your mother did not show love toward you because you came home one day and smashed a window, and she rejected you as a result of this. Let us suppose you are predisposed to feeling rejected, and as a result of this experience, you react with sadness that your mother has rejected you. Children recover very quickly from this feeling of rejection. The brain of a child does not retain the memory of rejection. Later in life, say when you are twenty years old, you are in love for the first time, and by accident you break a window at your girlfriend's house, and she is upset. This will immediately create an association with your past memory of rejection, which may trigger an overemotional reaction in you as a defense. Your girlfriend asks you later on why you behaved like that, as it was not necessary to get quite so emotional.

Illnesses can also trigger reaction: for example, there are people who, on being diagnosed with cancer, start to see the world differently because they feel released from their usual obligations. Some of them remember being unhappy as a child. In others, some of whom remember their childhood as happy, the cancer triggers depression and feelings of hopelessness. So depression cannot be explained in such a simplistic way. It is always more helpful to look for a possible trigger than a cause.

It is also important to look into the connection between what is present and what is manifested. Everything is always present on different levels, but as the brain can only process a certain amount of information, most remains unmanifest. With awareness we begin to realize how much more there is to learn and discover about life. For example, an illness involves a gradual build up of energy blockage, which takes time. The brain starts very early on in life building up this energy blockage, which eventually impedes awareness and prevents us from having all our energy present for observation.

The limits of manifestation

So all may not be manifest or available for us in ordinary experience, but everything is present. If we constantly focus only on what is manifest and say that this is the sum total of awareness, then we miss the point. We need to be a step ahead of what is manifest; we need to be in our state of being. What is present must always be more than what appears in its manifestation – the mystics called this holism. There is the whole, but some of it is hidden or obscured by our identification with theory or convention, by our cynicism and addiction to security or what we think we know. But if we see only what is manifest, we miss the surrounding atmosphere of what is present.

At this point, it is important to remember that awareness plus description is mind or brain consciousness. Whenever we create labels or describe things – the opposite process to depersonalization – we create mind consciousness.

Awareness with the absence of description is direct observation. Again, awareness does not require us to have input using our knowledge, to describe, measure and compare. Consider the very simple example of listening to music, which is something that does not require a description in order for it to register in your being. Listening to a piece of music requires awareness, but if at the same time you try to describe what you are hearing, you will not enjoy the music. When this happens the experience becomes cut off from us – it is no longer a part of our process; it has become an artificial independent identity. Sadly, this is exactly how many of us relate to our bodies – we split off our mind from our body by focusing on our body and describing what we feel. Body-mind cannot be separated. Feelings are manifested through the body, but feelings are more than the body. Whenever we describe something happening in the body, we block the flow of energy in the body. It slows down the flow. Exactly the same process occurs whenever we create so-called consciousness, and the flow gets broken.

So we need to learn to be aware without description. Consciousness is not the issue. As the Buddha said, the hardest step of detachment is to detach from consciousness. In reply to the question "Will every person reach enlightenment?" the Buddha answered that when we have reached and understood enlightenment, enlightenment is no longer an issue. Being conscious of enlightenment is still part of the ego.

What he is saying is that to be aware of enlightenment calls for a description, and a description of something creates a separation, which in turn creates a slowing down of the flow of energy. Whenever we cannot describe something, we are in a space of atmosphere without consciousness.

No consciousness as out-of-body consciousness

If we can rest in an atmosphere, as, for example, in the feeling of the space within a church that is different but we cannot quite say how, we are in a place of out-of-body or no consciousness. The atmosphere and the movement of the process of being in the atmosphere becomes the process of letting go of description – the act of depersonalization.

If we step into an energy field and try to feel and describe what we feel at the same time, we will never fully feel it. The description creates blindness and obstructs the possibility of direct observation. We cease to feel once we start describing. The moment I describe my wife, for example, I cannot feel love. Description kills the atmosphere. If we are with someone who has just died, there is nothing specifically different about the body of the person before and after death. The only difference is in how their energy field, or their qualities, are anchored into the body over the region of the heart center or chakra. After death the energy body is no longer anchored in the body – it is just present in the room. It has not changed, but we experience it differently, and we will find it difficult to describe the difference. When we stop describing, personalizing and labelling, we are in the atmosphere, which always means being in touch with the qualities. Here we can begin the pro-

cess of melting, blending, giving up our sense of distance between ourselves and others, giving up the notion of separation.

We know about the body being form, which basically means that it can
defend itself. The I is time and therefore cannot defend itself, and
attempting to do so is an illusion. We believe we need to create boundaries or defense mechanisms and are horrified at any intrusion into our
personal space, at the possibility of not having a gap between me and
you. Ending separation does not mean that we give up our space, however – in fact, the space is essential in order for the melting process to
take place.

Being in flow
Melting is not the same as dissolving. Dissolving marks the end of
being conscious. Creating a movement where two things are melting
together means that we can no longer describe what is or is not dissolving. This is the principle of being in the atmosphere. For example,
if you worry that by entering into a relationship and giving yourself
totally to it that your I, your body and your being will dissolve, it will
be difficult to create an atmosphere in which to really feel the other
person, to really feel loving toward them.

The same applies in a therapeutic situation. Many psychotherapists and
classical psychoanalysts believe in keeping a certain distance from clients – not shaking hands with clients or calling them by their first name
or even talking in a simple friendly way is still common. It is often felt
that distance is necessary to avoid too much transference. But across
this distance, how can we put ourselves in the other person's shoes,
which is the only way to feel compassion and empathy, to really feel
and understand someone's suffering?

For example, if someone has severe and chronic pain, we might feel
sad for the person because we can see that they are in pain, but can we
really feel their pain? If we do not become that person, how can we

feel their pain? Even if we become that person, it will be difficult to fully feel their pain. However, if we can be in the atmosphere of the pain, we may not actually feel it, but we can sense how the person might be feeling. To do this we need to radically destroy description – in the words of Lao Tsu, we have to "be the flow." This simply means that there is never a point at which we can claim to have arrived. Whenever we become aware of something, it has already flowed along a little further.

Or as Heraclitus put it, "You can never step twice in the same river." Therefore, to give a description of the molecules of the water around your feet is unhelpful and is only breaking the flow. So in putting an end to description, the depersonalization process creates atmosphere. We stop describing and become the process, and when we become the process there is no more distance. There is no more description of fear; there is *I am the fear*, and in that there is the creation of an atmosphere. Depersonalization shows us that awareness is possible without description.

When there is awareness without description, there is not only an enlarging of manifestation, as everything is always present, but we are also in direct observation where there are no causes, only triggers. When the description stops, the atmosphere is suddenly there. The moment we begin to describe the quality, the energy of the quality slows down. Sadness cannot be understood through consciousness, awareness and description. What you are reading now is description, which is like pointing to the moon. Focus not on the finger, but on looking for the moon – otherwise, you might mistake the description of sadness for sadness itself.

So what is sadness? What is this tremendous energy that can create fear and anger when it is personalized or described? Aggression is a symptom of fear, and fear is a symptom of sadness. If we want to really understand aggression or fear, then we have to understand sadness.

Standing by the bridge

If we want to get to the depth of anything, we have to peel it like an onion, layer by layer, until we reach the heart, working very consciously and precisely. At the same time we need to keep in mind that the bits that remain undescribed while we are engaged in this process form the best instrument for understanding sadness. By seeing clearly what is present, we can often come face-to-face with what is not present, at which point we stop.

Imagine yourself standing on one side of a bridge. It does not matter under what condition or with what sort of feelings. You are just standing on the shore on one side of a bridge, while on the other side there is the landscape of love. On the other side you see paradise, the atmosphere of love. However, you cannot cross the bridge; something simply stops you from crossing to the other side. You do not want to discuss it or understand it – you are just standing there unable to cross the bridge, and you can see that on the other side there is love. The only awareness you have is that there is love. There is not a single human being, regardless of their history, who does not feel sadness when they arrive at this point of not being able to cross the bridge and of no longer being able to describe it.

Sadness exists when there is the absence of doing and knowing. When you are aware that there is no way of doing, no way of achieving, no way of any possible action, not even the action of fear and anger, then there can be sadness. You will not be able to die without it. Dying is first the movement of the realization that while you are within this body you cannot reach paradise. Then comes the movement of the realization that all your ideas and knowledge are part of the barrier to crossing the bridge.

After that follows the realization that if you tried to let go of the body, thoughts and mind, the process of letting go is a doing process and therefore will not help you cross the bridge. With this realization comes sadness, and before you know it you are over the bridge. You cannot walk over that bridge because it would be an act of doing. You cannot describe ways or solutions for crossing the bridge because this would also be an act of doing.

It is this sudden absence of doing that creates the tremendous energy of sadness. If this is an accurate description of how things are, then sadness is stillness. This direct stillness happens through not personalizing or describing. It happens when there is an absence of doing but not from stopping the act of doing. This is a classical paradox whereby the mind cannot stop doing, as this would be a description of how to stop doing which would be a form of doing. The not doing follows automatically and naturally, like listening to music; it is pure awareness. Through depersonalization we can say that sadness is immediately transformed into stillness.

In this you feel compassion rather than sadness. The sadness is present, but it is not manifest. As long as the sadness is identified as sadness, it will not be a force of transformation. The reason for this is that the mind quickly turns sadness into a description of self-pity or toward an object; for example, the sadness that follows the death of someone will not create a transformation.

You have to see it from the inside. There is no way of understanding this through the description. Do not cling to the description. In sadness there is the absence of any doing. When there is no doing, there is direct stillness.

Full of emptiness

When sadness is transformed into stillness, we no longer feel the sadness; there is just the breathtaking emptiness that the mystics often refer to. This is not emptiness devoid of anything, but one where there is a kind of totality. It is filled with energy, that is not directed toward any action, – energy that is used for nothing. This energy, which is full but is not used for any specific action, is compassion. Although compassion always includes sadness, it does not manifest as sadness: we do not feel sad. It is sadness and stillness that transforms the ego and the mind. When the mind is transformed, part of the brain is changed. There is not an absence of ego – we have not stopped our mind working, but the mind has simply changed. We find that the cortex is more active, and the brain reacts in a more holistic way. This "new ego" is active, but it is operating differently.

This new ego carries love. We have now crossed the bridge. It is not love that transforms the ego. Love is the manifestation of the transformation. First, there has to be sadness and stillness, followed by the transforming of the mind, and then comes love in action. The concept that love is capable of transforming the ego is incorrect because it is based on description.

Love is the manifestation of the new ego, the new mind, the new brain. The beauty is that it can happen in two ways. In the Buddhist tradition one school of thought says that to achieve enlightenment takes time, and another says enlightenment can happen in an instant. There is something very simple in this – the movement toward sadness that transforms to stillness and allows one to cross the bridge happens in many of us just for a second and then disappears. This is when we feel completely in touch with the atmosphere and at peace with everything. It can also happen totally and suddenly, rendering us totally transformed, but for most of us it does not happen in one fell swoop. For most people what happens is that there is an increase in brain activity; the mind is totally in the new ego, and then it breaks down again into the old pattern.

The danger of understanding
It really does not matter in which way it happens, as long as it does happen. Imagine you are in a state of sadness – and remember that sadness is the absence of doing. You might then initiate a process of describing how you are not in a state of anger, nor in a state of fear. You may then go on to feel that you must be on the right track. However, all of this will throw you out of stillness again. The moment you begin to describe sadness, it cannot move to stillness. It cannot be-

come a transformative force. The description will immediately pull it back to the level of fear or aggression.

For example, there is the kind of sadness that you can see in people who think they understand something, like those who believe in the absurd Christian theory that we can only be free through suffering. When we start to feel sad for others out of this motivation, we are in serious danger of doing nothing other than building up the old ego. Here there is no change in energy or in the way our brain functions. Sadness does not require any doing. Just as listening to music is awareness without description, sadness is also awareness without description. Whenever we are totally present we are not even aware of the sadness, the stillness and the compassion that we feel. We are not aware of crossing the bridge at all.

Martin Buber, one of the great German mystics, said that if we cannot suffer for the world, we do not know what compassion is. But to carry the cross and be aware that we carry the burden of the world is ugly to behold – it is the act of carrying the cross while being joyful that is enlightenment. So what is the nature of sadness? It is difficult for the mind to just remain in sadness. The mind will always be on the look-out for ways and means to *achieve* sadness and for hints and clues as to whether it is on the right track.

Back in touch

What brings us to this level of not being constantly in fear? What is the movement that takes us away from the fear and back to sadness? Remember that fear is a way of escaping sadness. The movement that takes us away from fear and back to sadness is that of being touched. This is different from compassion, which occurs once we are already with sadness – sadness, in its emptiness, is compassion. Being touched is the movement of forgetting the I, the ego – which means forgetting the need to describe – and the expansion of boundaries.

We can only be touched, when we are not defending – when there are no more defenses. We can only defend something that we have created as an entity by forming a description. Defending our ego does not really help transform the ego, it only increases its strength.

When boundaries are dissolved within the brain by not defending, it creates a tremendous input of serotonin. Many of us nowadays take medication or herbal remedies for depression that aim to increase levels of serotonin. However, the reason this may not be as effective as it could be is that much of the serotonin gets consumed in the act of defending the ego. We cannot change fundamentally, and the depression will not go away just by taking serotonin. It may help us to feel better, but the moment we stop taking it we drop back again into our depression.

Being touched is not possible while we are consumed with fear. When we cling to fear we cannot be touched, and we might even try to avoid being touched physically. If a friend tells you that she is afraid she will fail an examination and you identify with it, you connect what's being said with your own experience. If you identify with something that is being said, you are escaping into memories and thoughts that automatically preclude being touched. This is actually closer to avoiding being touched.

Being touched is the absence of description. To be touched you would need to experience the fear of being a failure, to share the fear. If you are then touched while in the process of experiencing this fear, you will be in contact with sadness. It is very difficult for the mind to be touched because being touched creates an absence of choice. The mind needs to have choices because having choices gives the impression or the illusion of being in control. On the level of the body this is appropriate and necessary.

If I were to play some music very loudly, for instance, and refused to allow anyone to leave the room even if they could not stand the noise, their immune system would drop dramatically by 30-40 percent. If they listened to the music for as long as possible but at the same time had the freedom to leave the room when they had had enough, their immune system would not drop at all. The problem starts once we get obsessive about something, because then we limit our choices. It is important to know the difference between the body, the mind and the psychospiritual level, which can be learned only through your own investigation. They interact with each other, but they are independent. On the psychospiritual level there cannot be any dependence on description – there has to be stillness.

Being touched is the absence of choice. The body, however, needs choice. The mind needs the illusion of choice; it does not in fact need real choice, but to be stable it needs the illusion of choice. On the psychospiritual level, choice is absent, and here we can see the connection to faith in Christian mystical terms. Faith in the mystical sense does not imply a blind belief in the God of whatever culture we are born into. A mystic knows that on the psychospiritual level there is no choice. We do not choose who we are going to be touched by – it could be someone who looks beautiful and agreeable or ugly and a little unpleasant, and it can happen when we least expect it in any situation.

Imagine yourself standing in the middle of a battlefield, in a neutral position between hundreds of Albanian refugees, on the one hand, and Serb soldiers on the other hand. When you see the suffering of the refugees, you are touched. When you see the suffering of the Serb soldiers or their families who may have just lost their sons, you are also touched. If you approach this situation from the point of view of cause and effect, you will be acting in an unjust way by being in favor of one side. For example, for a poor family of refugees, the Serbs are the cause of their misery. Or if you are a Serb, you will attribute the cause of the suffering to something else. If we can leave the cause out of all of this, we will be touched as much by the Serb child who loses her father in the course of defending his country as we would be by an Albanian driven out of her home.

Being touched has nothing to do with logic or judgment; it does not involve choice or ideas about right or wrong. Similarly, sadness has no rules, ideologies or descriptions. It is helpful to cultivate a state of being, therefore, where there is an absence of time. As we have seen, the I is time, and our feelings need to be totally separated from content, history or interpretation so that only the process of observation is left. When we feel touched, we move from fear to sadness. This is the nature of sadness, and in sadness we come into stillness and love.

CHAPTER 15

Out of Time and into the Heart

All of this means that we need to change our attitudes radically if we want to become free. With our rational minds we may ask why qualities exist at all. Without going into philosophy, religion or even science, we can see by direct observation that the answer to this question has to do with evolution.

We cannot observe God, but we can see something very simple in nature as each flower tries to blossom and fulfill its potential and each fruit tree tries to create fruit. Each seed has its pattern of energy, its fundamental evolutionary movement, which means it has a clear purpose – its reason for being – which is to become what it holds within itself. Clearly, evolution is the movement of becoming, not in the sense of knowledge or achievement but in blossoming into that which is dormant within us. In bringing fruit out of the tree, and in the flower bud that wants to open, we can see the movement of love.

The process of love

Each one of us is nothing other than the movement of love itself, and the qualities are the instruments through which this love is manifested. Each individual has different ways of manifesting the movement of love, but we are all involved in a general movement of nature trying to blossom, to share and to get in touch with that which is more than what is manifesting. Even the body is constantly trying to get in touch with others.

A body that can touch and be touched by others has a looseness and radiance about it. The immune system of someone who is touching and is being touched is much stronger than someone who does not have or does not want this kind of contact. Children are like the opening of a flower, a perfect example of the movement toward love. The transformative force driving evolution is in fact love. Energy, like evolution, is nothing other than love.

The movement of love is an unfolding, which is a different process from gradual growth. It unfolds with the help of the brain, which acts as a transmitter, an intermediate or a go-between. You may be asking how the human mind, if it is structured in misery and limitation, can become free. The point is that freedom is our true nature, which has become obscured and forgotten. We can see how every biological system is interconnected, so for instance each flower is not only blossoming in an attempt to fulfill its own destiny but is at the same time playing a part in the wider cycle of nature. If we spent more time watching what happens in nature we would realize what possibilities exist for us to radically change how our minds work.

How does a caterpillar, for example, transcend its being to become a butterfly? If we were to ask a caterpillar if it could become a butterfly, the caterpillar would say it was impossible. The caterpillar would be right because as a caterpillar it can only answer from the perspective of its caterpillar consciousness, and in order for transformation to happen, its caterpillar consciousness has to die. As we have seen, however, dying is not a process that happens only at the end of our lives when our body-mind is rearranged. With biological death nothing really dies – the structure just gets rearranged. True dying happens when our mind starts to see that it is not needed on certain other levels – for example, the psychospiritual level. The feeling level has no need to be attached, to grasp, to understand, and this is when the mind becomes a butterfly or becomes conscious of its true nature, which is revealed as an evolutionary process. Just as the seed carries the tree within it and from the tree comes the fruit, the body-mind can be seen to be nothing other than the seed.

We all make the common mistake of thinking that once we have grown up we have fulfillled our purpose, but in fact we have only just become the seed. As the seed, our mind consciousness has to die in order to become the fruit-bearing tree. Evolution in humans, plants and animals is all based on this movement away from the body-mind.

Energy and flow
In the Chinese classic the *Tao Te Ching*, Lao Tzu used water as a metaphor for energy, love and the flow of life. Imagine a river in which the water represents the qualities, our true nature. The qualities represent the manifestation of the flow of love. Then imagine an earthquake. The earthquake represents the creation of body-mind, the birth of consciousness. Things only become conscious when they get structured in form and time, so with the emergence of the earthquake we are in form and time. Remember that the body is form; the I, or the ego, is time. As the earthquake begins to move, the flow of the river stops; the river becomes blocked, and at this point we can see something very significant happen.

The flow of the river is now blocked, yet it will not stop trying to find a way through the blockage until it has either moved around the barrier created by the earthquake or through it. The water will always triumph in the end because it is softer than the obstruction. The qualities will always be present. This is where the symbolism of reincarnation comes from. If we consider it on the simple level of understanding birth and rebirth, then as long as the water has not found its way back to the source it will persist. It will go on trying and searching until the flow is reestablished, until we reach, in the words of the Buddha, a state of enlightenment or an awakening. Only when the flow has been reestablished do we come to the end of normal consciousness, the consciousness that is structured in the I, me and mine.

Just before awakening we will be able to see that the simple processes on which nature and everything else is based are exactly the same. There is no culture, for example, that does not display aggression. Aggression is a symptom of fear, which in turn is a symptom of sadness, and sadness is a symptom of love. Sadness provides the bridge to love. Every other emotion or behavioral trait is just description. Jealousy or greed is a description of a specific form of aggression and therefore can be related back to fear and sadness. Humans are much simpler than we like to admit. If we look at the beauty and the simplicity of it all, we find that our sense of individuality begins to fade away. The mind makes life complicated because in doing so we give ourselves an individual structure. This confers uniqueness, our very own self, unlike any other. Real beauty, however, is not something unique – it is simple, free and occurs universally.

The limits of psychology

To arrive at this point of appreciation of who we are, we have to see that we are more than psychological theory attributes to us. Freud's concept of the unconscious, for example, which still influences much of modern psychotherapy and is believed to contain all that is dark and hidden in our nature, is similar to the Christian belief that we are all naturally sinful and need to repent before our suffering will end and we reach the kingdom of heaven. We do not need to limit ourselves in this way.

The seed that defines and labels itself and is content with that definition places itself in a particular frame and never becomes a thing of beauty. There are many possible ways in which our potential might unfold. We are different in society at large from how we are with a close friend or when we are alone. We have different selves contained within us at the same time. Allow the quality, the atmosphere, to shine on all of the selves. There is nothing wrong with having different selves as long as they are able to coexist harmoniously within the whole, which is the atmosphere of the qualities.

What we regard as our weaknesses are simply a warning that we are not in touch with our true consciousness, and we need to just observe the warning and let it guide us. If we did not feel pain on the body level, we would not be able to survive. Similarly, the weaknesses are a form of mental pain, and they are signalling that we have created a distance in our relationship to the source. If we limit ourselves to psychology, we cut ourselves off from the possibility of interaction with others.

Listening to the cries of the heart

In both Buddhism and Christianity we are urged to practice forgiveness. In Buddhism the bodhisattva Avalokitesvara is also known in female form as Kwan Yin in the Far East, or "she who listens to the cries of the heart." Each one of us can be a bodhisattva, one who listens to the cries of the heart, some of the time. In the *Heart Sutra*, which is regarded as the essence of Buddhist teaching, we learn that the observation of a wrong action or mistake is like listening to the cries of the heart and that it shows that we have been out of touch with our true nature. So we need to learn how to listen to the cries of the heart. Jesus referred to the same thing in saying that the process is fundamentally one of forgiveness because each wrong action is created out of misunderstanding and lack of contact with the source of our being. In the process of forgiveness we move away from the past. Nothing else is needed.

In the Second Noble Truth, the Buddha points out that emotions and feelings are our natural response to problems, difficulties and suffering. We can see only too clearly that the world is full of problems and injustices, and what is happening in the world is a mirror of what is happening in us and in our relationships with each other. Naturally whenever there is an earthquake or whenever we have a problem, the emotions come into play, and we try to escape from the problem. Deep inside we know that our nature is to be connected with other people.

It is through connecting with other people that we can put an end to suffering. Both the Buddha and Jesus taught that we end suffering by being in touch with the cries of the heart that come from sadness and with the quality of compassion. It is important to nurture the realization that sadness is not something negative that we need to avoid in our lives. Whenever we are aggressive it shows that we are running away from a relationship with fear. When we experience fear – and remember this relates only to psychological fear – we are trying to block out the crying of the heart. Without sadness, we cannot cross the bridge to love and on the way cultivate compassion, which is the movement of love combined with sadness.

When we do not deeply care for ourselves or for others, and caring includes sadness, there is never the flowering of love in the sense of bliss. In Buddhist teachings the Sanskrit word *samatha* means to stop, and we can see that flowering of our being can only happen if we can stop reacting to things on the mental level. The caterpillar or the seed in the process of transformation is not fighting what is happening; it is absorbed in the process of becoming something else, a different form, another expression of the source. It is just receiving; it is just in a state of direct observation. This is the kind of intelligence we need to nurture.

Can we stop reacting? When we feel angry (and there is nothing wrong with anger), can we stop for a moment in order to see that anger is in fact fear? If we then express the anger, if we live the anger, we can never see beyond it to the fear. When we feel fear instead of reacting and interpreting, trying to shut it out by keeping busy, trying to justify it or repress it, can we see that behind the fear there is sadness? Transformation is only possible if we do not react to the symptom; whenever we give an interpretation to sadness, for example, it becomes self-pity. The personalization of any movement is what creates the problem. If we stop trying to interpret the sadness and just see the process, or the movement of it, we find ourselves crossing the bridge to love. We start to unfold again, just as the seed begins to open and sprout, moving closer to our essential nature, to the source that is our reason for being.

Approaching our true nature

Many of us live our lives caged like animals whose real purpose is to run free and wild and who naturally become dangerous in captivity, or birds who want only to fly but spend their lives with clipped wings. We become caged in the prison of the ego, which is essential for our functioning on the biological and biopsychological consciousness level. What is appropriate on one level, however, cannot be used as an instrument on another; this is how misunderstandings and mistaken beliefs arise, like regarding the ego as the root of our problems or seeing the body as an impurity.

We need to begin to think and examine things for ourselves. The Buddha told his followers not to believe what he said but to observe and inquire for themselves. We need to use our minds to think about all of this and also to get in touch with our essential nature. In trying to find out how can we approach our qualities, we have seen that the ego, the I, is the content of the past, or our knowledge, and is the process of describing and identifying with our experiences. We give a description and an identification to each of our experiences as we learn, and in the process of learning, each time the experience is repeated, our brain requires less energy to carry out the task. For example, when we learn to drive a car, at first we are very cautious and aware of each action, but in time the driving becomes automatic, and our brain can concentrate on other things.

On the feeling level, however, if we try to describe or identify experiences, we create a barrier. For example, imagine you have spent the evening with someone you feel you love. You have a wonderful time, and at the end of the evening you say, "I love you." Let's say that the person goes home because it is late and it is early on in your relationship. When you are on your own, you create an identification with the experience by giving it a description – you may say that you love the person because of such and such, and you try to describe your feelings. You try as best as you can to describe what you mean by the love you feel. On meeting the person the next day, if you then try to duplicate the experience of the previous evening, you are bound to be disappointed.

A similar thing happens when we have read a book that we like very much and then see the film adaptation of it. We nearly always come away from the movie disappointed. Those who have not read the book, on the other hand, may like the movie but subsequently feel disappointed on reading the book. Or everybody raves about a movie that you find to be a disappointment. If you had gone to see it before hearing the rave reviews, you may have had a different experience. This is how experience creates a limitation.

In the same way, clinging to experiences on the feeling or atmosphere level limits the possibility for love. Love is always new. The qualities are always new. If we create a painting or a piece of music that is successful and we then cling to this success, more and more limitation occurs. In psychology this is known as burnout, and the soul starts to bleed. Here the idea of the experience becomes more important than the new experience. That is why Krishnamurti said, "In order to live you have to be prepared to die to each moment." Not you physically, not your mind, but the experience has to die or be let go. Can you see that each experience, on being given a description or identification, becomes an expectation? Can you see that the expectation is limiting and takes us further away from our potential? Any expectation that is based on an experience closes down the possibilities or the potential for love, and it limits the possibility of developing a relationship to the qualities.

To go back to the seed metaphor, imagine that the seed can see and that it is possible to show it the tree that it is to become – say, an apple tree. The seed looks at it and then maybe tries to imagine what it must be like to become an apple tree. If the apple tree shown to the seed is a rather small one, the seed identifies with it and limits its potential to become a much bigger apple tree. There is an important distinction here between experience on the body-mind level, the biological level and the psychospiritual level, and this is why we need to cultivate awareness.

People suffering from Alzheimer's disease, for example, can no longer rely on experience; they are alive, but often living in misery. Their experience has nothing to do with their survival and is not necessary for the body-mind. Love is not necessary for survival. Identification or description have no place in the slow feelings of happiness, love or bliss, otherwise we simply create a prison for ourselves. Learning to see things in this way does not require us to change anything; we just need a shift of perspective for things suddenly to look different. The seed does not need to become something else; it just needs to stop holding on to being a seed, to stop being conscious of itself as only a seed.

Chopping wood

When we are in the flow, we may feel good for no particular reason – there is a feeling of lightness, of being uplifted and having peace of mind or *samadhi*. In this state we are the flow of energy, and so we do not experience feeling happy because the feeling of happiness would mean that someone is aware of being happy, and once the mind comes into play we then immediately create duality. The energy would again be diverted into being conscious of being happy. The flow of feeling good remains for as long as we do not try to label it.

The moment we begin to describe it, the flow stops. In reply to the question "What is before and after enlightenment?" the Zen masters said, "Before enlightenment – chopping wood; after enlightenment – chopping wood." Enlightenment does not just give us the feeling of total bliss, love and happiness; it gives us the movement toward simplicity and humbleness, which the mind calls boredom.

There is nothing special going on; it just feels very natural. There will be no feelings of ecstasy; we will feel very simple, which means that we have no need to label what is happening.   In the age of the return of the guru, many people now call themselves mystics and are constantly publicizing how much they are in bliss and connected with God. A true mystic does not look especially enlightened or spiritual. The Buddha, when asked if he was enlightened, replied simply, "I am awake." Rarely do we find the enlightened claiming to be enlightened – it is more likely that on being asked if they are enlightened, they will say no.

Being in flow instead becomes a state of being, and your state of being is only experienced by an outside source, by some other person. You will not be aware of how loving you are, but others will find you loving toward them. What is happening is that the mind constantly wants to be aware of the qualities, but the qualities are manifest only when we are not aware of them, when we have become the qualities, when we are the atmosphere of the qualities.

Using our brain consciousness, we can observe our mind; we can observe the body, thoughts and feelings. If we shift our perspective we come into the region of what cannot be grasped, the witness that can never be reached, touched or understood. We can try to interpret, but our interpretations depend on how we perceive it, and the moment we try to name it, it fades away. We are in the region of that which is always present within us, which can be called God or simply the timeless observer.

If we bring our awareness to something, we are in a process without having to give it a description. A process without description cannot be structured in time; we are absorbed in something and we lose track of time, but we will have been aware all the way through. If we paint a picture and are focused on how we want it to look and what people will think of it, we may have been deeply concentrating on what we are doing, but we have not been in a state of awareness. In a state of total absorption we are in surrender, to put it in Zen terms; we become the process and lose our sense of time, which, as Einstein said, is all relative. If we are deeply in love with someone, an hour passes as if it were a minute, but if we sit on a hot stove, a minute will feel like an hour. Awareness then is the absence of description; it is flow, and the body-mind stops doing and becomes a carrier of energy and of the qualities. The body-mind is like a candle, while the qualities are the flame. Through the activation of the qualities the body-mind lights up, so to speak.

So when you are in the process of love and you just have the awareness without the description, something tremendous happens. You come to stillness. Awareness without description naturally creates stillness. When consciousness is awareness with description, at this point brain/mind consciousness comes into play – for example, when we try to describe the stillness.

Stillness and love
One of the reasons that so many relationships fall apart is because the mind does not know how to deal with this process of stillness. The words we use when we "fall in love" reinforce our earlier concept of love being something we cannot make happen or do anything about. The first four months of being in love are driven by the body, primarily by the whole hormonal system. After this initial high we have to move to love. After a little longer a certain calmness sets in, and at this point people become fearful that the love may be fading away. This is only because there is no longer any clinging. As we have seen, the mind is an adrenaline addict and therefore feels uncomfortable in a state of calmness.

This is similar to what happens when we start meditating and arrive at a point of calmness and stillness. The mind gets worried that something is wrong because your I, your ego, is no longer busy trying to get attention from your partner. This is the real meaning of being together in a loving way. A relationship has to move into this stillness in order to survive, and the relationship you have with yourself is exactly the same. Each relationship you have is only a mirror of the relationship that you have with yourself.

If we are constantly fighting against our weaknesses, how can there be stillness? If we always want to know which qualities we are exhibiting at any one moment, how can there be stillness? This is the paradox, of course. We have to know our qualities, but we cannot control when or how they present. Other people can be our feedback system to indicate whether or not the qualities are in action.

The Christian concept of humility is important here. Is it possible for you to start to be in touch with your qualities, to know your qualities and then just leave them to manifest? For example, let us say one of your qualities is softness. If people close to you then identify with it, they create an experience and therefore an expectation. Whenever the softness is not present, they may be troubled. Even worse than that, through creating the expectation as a result of the experience (which is the past), they create a duality. You are then constantly observing whether or not you really have the quality of softness and whether you are able to deal with the softness. You therefore split yourself in two, and there is never enough energy for the quality as such to manifest fully.

Practical guidance
So is there a practical way around this? The mind always wants practical ways of achieving things. The mind would prefer techniques, but as we have said before, techniques do not take us to stillness. However, we can try to give the mind some help. Here are a few guidelines, or rather attitudes, which are born out of stillness, that will help you to get in touch with the qualities without being conscious of them.

Try to bear in mind that whatever you experience, whatever you may feel at the moment, is actually a part of the past. The first thing the mind has to see is that whatever you perceive in the moment is the past, and in clinging to the past you block the flow toward the future. The seed holding on to its seedness would never become the tree.

We need to try to be constantly aware without description, which will help us not to react in difficult situations. For example, when you are in the presence of someone who is shouting at you, wait three seconds before reacting, and you will be amazed by what happens. After three seconds you may find that the person who was shouting has moved on, perhaps to the point where they realize that there is no point in being angry. If you react to the very first expression of anger, the other will continue as if their process of being angry is a reality. By stopping and waiting, the angry person has a chance to move to the second stage of seeing the consequences of his or her actions. Students of martial arts are taught that whenever something comes toward them and they give it space, the impact of the energy starts to diminish.

Use this method to increase your awareness that whatever you perceive at the moment is the past and to help you see that whatever you feel coming from someone else is also a part of the past. In doing this you create space, which creates a possibility for the atmosphere to change. Use the same method for yourself when you feel anger or fear – remind yourself that it is already a part of the past; stop and give it space so that the whole structure can change by itself. Never try to change the structure yourself with the mind. The mind that has created the aggression in the first place cannot really change it; the mind can only repress it, which does not solve the problem.

Anger-fear-sadness-love

Although we do not all look the same or act in the same way, we are all alike in our processes. So whenever you become aggressive or angry, even if the anger is totally justified, just observe it for what it is – a symptom of fear. It does not matter if anger can be justified or not; there is not a single phase of aggression on the psychospiritual level that is not a symptom of fear. When Jesus is described as going into the temple angry, under the anger he is afraid that the temple is not being used for its true purpose. Whenever you feel fear coming, try to use your awareness to see that all fear is sadness. For example, it is not that you are angry that someone does not love you; it is that you are afraid of not being loved. In fact, you are not even really afraid of not being loved; you are simply sad that in being rejected by another you are deprived of the opportunity to express your love. So even if your fear looks totally real, it is a symptom of sadness. If you escape from being with the sadness, the fear will return, and if you escape the fear, you will experience aggression once more.

Just being with the sadness without personalizing it and turning it into self-pity, we find it does not remain as sadness; it moves automatically to love. Real understanding is born, not out of the intellect but of a deep feeling of caring. When someone dies and there is absolutely no possibility of intervening, we realize that in this sadness, which cannot be personalized and in which there is absolutely no hope, the feelings of sadness vanish into a feeling of bliss. A holy atmosphere prevails. When we are totally with sadness, it always transforms to love.

Let the process happen

Whenever we are dealing with others, it is helpful if we try to bring our interaction onto the level of feelings or the atmosphere, where we stop all the interpretation and description. To me, most relationships resemble what happens when tourists come to Switzerland. They go into the mountains and take a lot of photographs but do not really spend time looking at the mountain – they really look at the mountain only when they get home! This is how we tend to look at relationships. We immediately describe someone in terms of whether or not we like them or whether we like their taste in clothes. This is all about giving the other a description – and remember that when someone says they do not like what you are wearing, they are only saying something about their own taste in clothes.

If you want to find out something about someone, ask not who they are but what they think about you, and their answer will tell you a lot about them. So we need to be in direct contact, but if we constantly describe what is happening, then we limit the possibility of what might be. There is no need to describe – the process itself is sufficient. We can reflect as much as we want to after the process. This is what the mind is for, but during the process do not interfere by bringing in the mind. Let whatever is happening happen by itself. Love does not need our help – it's we who are in need of love's help.

We also need to stop asking the question "Why?" "Why am I like this, why do I have this weakness?" Instead, look at how things happen. Don't ask why you are jealous, but how your feelings of jealousy arise and how you express them or not. What is the process of jealousy? If I am afraid, I need to look at how this feeling of fear manifests in my mind. What is the process of it? What arouses the fear? What does it respond to? What gets in the way of it ceasing? In this way we reach the root of our thinking processes. The content of our thoughts changes from moment to moment, from culture to culture, from situation to situation. There is no need to know the content – the source of thought is the beauty that thoughts are the flowering of consciousness. Consciousness is the process of awareness and description; thought is the movement of describing. That is what all our spiritual teachers throughout history have meant by dealing with thought. If we focus on the content rather than the movement of thought, we will always be a prisoner of the content.

As we have seen, we have three thought structures and two thought processes. If we have six to seven thoughts at the same time, who is going to decide which thought is dominant and which thought we should be more conscious of? Thinking is a tool we can use to understand the world, but it is impossible to use it to understand ourselves because if we ask who or what am I, we become trapped in illusion, identification and attachment.

Try to be aware that each feeling is born out of a thought, so we have to start to look at each of our feelings, which in the end are all based on either aggression, fear, sadness, bliss or happiness. Try to see the connection between thought and feeling without bringing in a description. When we see that each feeling is created by a thought, and if we do not focus on getting to the source of the content, but instead to the source of the thought, we find stillness.

Stillness and heart communication

In stillness we come back to "out-of-body consciousness" which is anchored in the spiritual center of the heart, not in the brain. The spiritual center is the area encompassing the heart and throat, and the throat chakra is the emotional center. In coming into contact with the spiritual center of the heart, we need to relearn the language of feelings on the heart level to be true to our nature, to feel whole again and connect with ourselves, each other and the world with our fullest potential as human beings. In learning how to contact the slow feelings of compassion, love, joy, inner peace, inner space and stillness, we rediscover what we have forgotten: that the heart is the connection to out-of-body consciousness, the source of stillness and possible transformation.

As we have seen, in Time Therapy, all the problems of the mind are based on time because thinking is always either in the memory (the past) or in expectation (the future), but the actual thought processes happen in the present. In all psychological problems, even in cases of acute trauma such as a car accident or an ongoing traumatizing situation in which a person loses perspective on life, the problem is attached to time and our identification with what is happening or has happened.

In learning how to step out of time – out of mind consciousness and its attachment to description, away from the activity of the brain – and into the out-of-body consciousness, psychological symptoms can be relieved as we begin to experience space, freedom and relaxation. As the flow or energy between the *heart-mind* and *heart-out-of-body* consciousness is reestablished, a huge shift in perspective and expansion becomes possible. So how can we learn how to step out of time?

Heart energy

Human behavior is the sum of body sensations, thoughts and feelings, and while much research has been done on the mind and brain, we are only just beginning to rediscover what the ancients knew – that the area around the heart, the heart center or chakra, radiates more energy than the brain and plays a greater role in our well-being than we think. The only place in the human mind-body system where there is no structure of time is in the region of the heart.

The physical heart, as we know, is vital to life; it pumps blood through the whole mind-body system, creating energy. The vibration rate of the brain is only zero to thirty cycles per second, whereas that of the heart is much higher at zero to one hundred cycles – almost forty times stronger than the brain vibration. The heart center has a biological relationship to the thymus gland, which is responsible for the immune system, and the physical heart produces hormones that influence the brain. Between our thoughts, feelings and body sensations there is a gap, a space, an emptiness, which we call the *zero factor*. Following each sensation, feeling or thought there is an impulse and then a reaction to that impulse, and again, between the impulse and reaction there is a space of emptiness or stillness.

Research has shown that something sensational happens when we start to observe this zero factor: the immune system increases by 20 percent during five minutes of practicing this observation. The health aura becomes more vital, and in the brain there is a significant increase in serotonin levels. With practice, as we observe the emptiness more and more, the gap becomes greater, and it is here that we can experience deep relaxation in its truest sense. In this stillness, we come into contact with the emptiness that contains everything, which is also the nothingness in which love is born, and here we connect with our heart energy.

In stillness love, compassion, bliss and inner peace follow naturally without any effort. What the Buddha called *tathata* or *suchness*, meaning "the buddha nature hidden in things just as they are," refers to the observation of this space of love. Every behavior can be traced back to compassion. The root of all behavior, even that which we might call bad or unacceptable behavior, is compassion – the movement of sadness and love at the same time. This includes having compassion for oneself.

If we can see this in our observation, our attitude and perspective on life changes, allowing us to feel forgiveness for the past and releasing our potential in the future. If we meet our enemy out of that emptiness, there is no urge for revenge and no attachment to past pain and suffering. We can see that the reason we suffer is because we would like to express love, to share and be loving. Reconnecting with our heart energy out of stillness, we find the possibility of an end to suffering.

Nourishing the heart

When the heart energy changes, it automatically influences brain activity. In order to change our behavior on a personal and global level then, we need to do more than learn how to think healthily or learn how to relax and practice our meditation. We need to reestablish the heart connection and bring our heart energy into our relationships with others and with ourselves.

How manifest the heart energy is in our daily life depends upon how much energy we channel into it. If we have cut ourselves off from the heart as a result of being hurt and are more familiar with pain and heartache than with love and joy, we have in effect cut ourselves off from our potential, from the qualities that are the real essence of our being. Despite the fact that over time we may have shut down the heart for our own perceived protection, the heart chakra does not need to be developed in any way, as it is always present. We still have the heart energy that we were born with, but we need to activate and nourish it so that it can function productively on the physical, emotional, mental and spiritual levels, and if we do this then the connection to the out-of-body consciousness increases.

Moving away from time

Time ceases only when you are simply in a movement away from yourself, as in the moments when you fall in love, for example, when there is no sense of time. Making a conscious effort of mind to reach this state, however, does not help the flow of energy to the heart. The process of wanting to change blocks energy. Wanting to change or wanting to do something splits energy and stops flow, reducing vitality. Wanting to change in fact creates time.

Naming what you want to change means you cannot observe it anymore. Interpretation is description, which is thinking. No interpretation, no description and no identification increases the heart energy. When there is no choice to be made, no way out to take, we find that time just goes. The heart can take over the energy of the brain when we stop interpreting what is happening, and energy can move through the heart to bring freedom and peace. When we do not want anything and are motivated just by the movement of giving, the heart energy starts to increase. If we just practice simply observing in the present without description, without any identification, we find ourselves in stillness and in flow. Flow means there is no beginning and no end and therefore no time to get in the way of love, bliss and stillness.

Into the flow of relationship

Ultimately, we need to learn how to create space physically and mentally in order to connect with the source of energy. Space itself has no movement, but movement happens in space, so creating space encourages the movement of energy. Moving away from the physical body does not mean being against the body, but the body needs space so that we can create a relationship between the different parts of our being – physical, subtle, etheric, heart, mind, feelings and thoughts. Think of a circle as a symbol of oneness, of a whole. What is most striking is that there is no beginning and no end; there is no time. Analyzing the circle has no meaning – in a cycle or circle there is no cause and effect, just an interrelationship, an interdependence.

When we are in total observation we have created a relationship, which has a transforming effect. Whenever we observe something, we immediately have an influence on it. Energy is transformed through being in a realationship with something, and relationship is observing. Be in total observation of your weakness or problem, therefore, and something will change as energy has been created in the stillness of observation.

If we take Lao Tzu's example of water as a metaphor for energy, love and the flow of life, we see that water can become ice or frozen energy, which is a symptom of illness or psychological problems. If we take the sun as a symbol of observation, or relationship, when we observe the ice it melts and moves back to water again. But if we take the ice and hit it, adding aggressive action to already frozen energy, and break it into pieces, it is still ice; it is still frozen energy now fragmented or split. When the pieces thaw out and become water again, it may be regarded as normal, but what we think of as normality is a long way from health, quality of life and well-being.

Letting the sun shine on the water as pure observation, we see that a transformation takes place as energy moves and shapes change. That is when we move from being normal to being healthy, and it can only happen through direct observation, creating a relationship to whatever is there, connecting with it without any interference and transforming the energy of it. Simply allowing ourselves to be in relationship or observation does not need effort, knowledge or understanding, and we do not need to feel secure about the outcome of our observation. As the Buddha said, all is observation, but do not be attached to the results of your observation.

Into insecurity and love

Reestablishing a flow of energy through observation and relationship means the ending of concepts. Concepts involve a thought process that does not allow you to be with your own heart in connection with yourself. With concepts there can be no stillness. Energy does not need security to create love and stillness. Flow has no security. Can you step into flow, into total insecurity?

Insecurity gives us a glimpse of stillness and the movement of love. Energy is transformed into thought by insecurity; thought is directed energy. Can your mind be totally insecure in order to move to stillness and love? You may be thinking that we feel secure only by thinking, but thought brings only the illusion of security; the only true security there is comes through stillness. Thoughts actually create insecurity, even though each thought is born, out of trying to avoid insecurity. Can you see that thought is created by trying to control insecurity? The mind tells us that we "should" control it, especially as part of this insecurity emerges as the energy of sadness moving through the heart. If we can just be with this sadness – not the personalized sadness of self-pity – we are on the bridge to love. At this point can you see how bringing in thought involves a constant movement of the past into the future, bringing in memory and experience and projecting it into the future?

Wisdom never creates a belief system because a belief system involves thought, and when we think there can be no observation. Observation is the ending of effort; it comes into being when you don't know and when there is no desire to control, no desire for identification. The beauty of the interconnecting dialogue of the circle then is that we can start from the points of love, stillness, observation or insecurity to connect to our heart energy.

The point of observation

It doesn't matter where we start in the circle in nourishing the heart energy, as it is all interconnected and interdependent. You can start with insecurity, but if you cannot bear the freedom of insecurity, you can start from the point of love. Love, however, is essentially the absence of security, which comes into being only if you simply observe without reaction. You cannot be with the heart through knowledge and understanding, which is why love does not transform the ego –

love is the manifestation of what lies beyond the ego. Or you can start with stillness, but if you are waiting for an answer to a question, you are not in stillness. Or you can start directly with observation because observation is part of our true nature.

How can we get to a state of observation without thinking about it? Only if we realize there is emptiness or absence of the mind, but then we are immediately in the realm of insecurity. We cannot avoid love, sadness or stillness because we all have at least moments or glimpses of emptiness where there is nothing. Psychological problems arise mainly because we constantly try to avoid the cycle of stillness, which creates tension and frustration and can lead to worsening of symptoms. All psychological problems are created by time, and it follows therefore that they can be solved or overcome by stepping out of time. The spiritual center of the heart is the anchor to the out-of-body consciousness and also the anchor of the timeless observer.

Into the heart center

When we find ourselves in a state where the content of thoughts is no longer the main focus, we are in insecurity, and there is the possibility of being with the spiritual center of the heart, the anchor to out-of-body consciousness or the timeless observer. When we move away from the body, the anchor becomes more vital and energized. Try as often as you can to be in touch with the spiritual center, not on the level of the body, but about thirty centimeters away from the heart area.

To be in stillness means being in total insecurity with no reaction, no knowing and total observation.

Observation is the absence of thought that wants to achieve, to change, to avoid insecurity.

Stillness and emptiness in movement become love.

The outcome of this is simplicity and humility. In insecurity enlightenment happens – the atmosphere of bliss, joy, peace and compassion. Here we are connected to the main source of love, which means that it does not matter even if you are not aware of it because the connection with the qualities is always there. It is essentially the energy of love. Love is movement out of stillness. It is the movement of evolution, of sharing, unfolding, flowering, becoming. You are the carrier of love and the qualities. This is what energy really means. Sharing is the ultimate movement of love, and only a world of sharing can be a truly peaceful world.

About the Author

Manuel Schoch was born in 1946 in Switzerland and from childhood has had the gift of being able to perceive energy fields or auras of people, including clairvoyant vision and audition of dead people, spirits and other entities. Throughout his life he has had various mystical experiences.

After school, Manuel went into farming for a few years. He then studied psychology in Switzerland and England, where he also refined his psychic and mediumship skills. He worked as the youngest editor for the Swiss television network and as personnel manager of a large communication company.

After several years of studying with the Danish healer Bob Moore, Manuel started his own work as an energetic therapist in 1971. He was the co-founder of the Analytic Center in Zurich and in 1974 he founded the *HiHo-Collective*, an anti-psychiatric institution.

The unfolding of Manuel's healing abilities led him to open the *Tune-in Center for Human Growth*, where in 1984 he started to express his qualities in public with talks, workshops and training programs.

Manuel Schoch has developed *Time Therapy* and *Out of Body Healing* and works with his own wisdom, clarity, compassion, humour and humbleness. His approach and style of teaching is both very simple and practical, ideally suited for modern day life.

Today, Manuel Schoch is the director of the *Tune-in Center for Time Therapy* based in Zurich, London and Athens. He teaches at the University of Zurich, bridging science and spirituality. He is also head consultant for the most recent research programs of the psychiatric department at Zurich University, where he looks for more modern and effective ways of treating depression and schizophrenia, and finds scientific evidence for his mystical perceptions.

One of Manuel's plans for the immediate future is a joint venture research program with the US Heffer Institute regarding the clinical use of drugs.

Manuel Schoch is married, has two sons and lives in Zurich. He regularly travels to teach in London, Athens and New York.

About Time Therapy

What is Time Therapy?
While traditional psychology seeks to explore and understand the self within its natural limits of space/time or cause/effect, spirituality is beyond all bounds.

With thirty years of careful observation of the human energy system, Manuel Schoch has developed Time Therapy as a direct and practical way to consciously integrate the potential of your quality aura into the realms of the body-mind and your everyday life.

Time Therapy, the bridging of psychology with spirituality, is a therapeutic perception based on the facts that:

• Everyone has qualities and needs to give attention to them rather than their weaknesses.

• The role of the past is not as important as we believe or make it out to be.

• We are more influenced by our fear of the future rather than our fear of the past, which means starting to take more responsibility instead of blaming the past.

• The majority of illnesses, especially psychological ones, are the result of having no more perspective.

• The expression of love is not dependent on first receiving love.

Why is it called Time Therapy?
The most common thing we know about time is not the wristwatch time but the cause-and-effect structure of time. What Time Therapy simply demonstrates is that there is no cause-and-effect structure.

Time Therapy shows us that we are more than the body-mind. We have all experienced a sense of this at certain moments in life when we lose all sense of time, when we really are connected to this expanded state of another bigger dimension – what Time Therapy refers to as out-of-body consciousness.

This is when we are truly in touch with and living our qualities or soul potential. Time Therapy shows us how to more easily and readily step out of time into the out-of-body consciousness state. This brings more perspective into our lives, whereby we can observe and feel what's going on within ourselves without the reactive reflex, based on fear, that commonly has imprisoned us and which stops the flow of energy and the ability to process and deal with situations and move on.

Being able to connect more with this expanded state, which we all have as part of our whole being, brings with it that inner peace, stillness and vitality that we all long for.

Addresses:

Tune in
Institut für Time Therapie
Seestrasse 561
8038 Zürich
Switzerland
0041 1 481 71 81
Tune-in@cybercity.ch
www.tune-in.ch
manuel.schoch@bluewin.ch

Tune in Center for Time Therapy
57 Harley Street
London W1G8QS
England
0044 207 636 42 89
www.timetherapy.co.uk

Tune in Center for Time Therapy
14 St.Georges Mews
London NW18XE
England
0044 207 586 58 56
sanita.hochhauser@btinternet.com

Tune in Center for Time Therapy
Stratigou Ionnou 18
11636 Athens
Greece
0030 10 752 1450
juliehardenberg@ath.forthnet.gr

Sentient Publications, LLC publishes books on cultural creativity, experimental education, transformative spirituality, holistic health, new science, ecology, and other topics, approached from an integral viewpoint. Our authors are intensely interested in exploring the nature of life from fresh perspectives, addressing life's great questions, and fostering the full expression of the human potential. Sentient Publications' books arise from the spirit of inquiry and the richness of the inherent dialogue between writer and reader.

Our Culture Tools series is designed to give social catalyzers and cultural entrepreneurs the essential information, technology, and inspiration to forge a sustainable, creative, and compassionate world.

We are very interested in hearing from our readers. To direct suggestions or comments to us, or to be added to our mailing list, please contact:

SENTIENT PUBLICATIONS, LLC
1113 Spruce Street
Boulder, CO 80302
303-443-2188
contact@sentientpublications.com
www.sentientpublications.com